A Primer on Innovation Theology

A Primer on Innovation Theology

Responding to Change in the Company of God

LANNY VINCENT

WIPF & STOCK · Eugene, Oregon

A PRIMER ON INNOVATION THEOLOGY
Responding to Change in the Company of God

Wipf & Stock
An Imprint of Wipf and Stock Publishers
199 W. 8th Ave., Suite 3
Eugene, OR 97401

www.wipfandstock.com

PAPERBACK ISBN: 978-1-5326-0879-7
HARDCOVER ISBN: 978-1-5326-0881-0
EBOOK ISBN: 978-1-5326-0880-3

Manufactured in the U.S.A.   DECEMBER 1, 2016

Unless otherwise noted, dictionary quotations and citations are from Leslie Brown, ed., *The New Shorter Oxford English Dictionary*, 2 vols. (Clarendon, 1993).

Contents

Prologue

Do We Really Need Another App for That?

BELIEF IN PROGRESS IS more widely held than frequently expressed, at least in North America. Though some might believe the new normal is more regress than progress, the mighty winds of American ingenuity, Horatio Alger and the entrepreneurial spirit still sweep over the face of the continent.

These winds perpetuate vague suppositions that somebody somewhere must be working on it—whatever it is—and will solve it, relieving us of our apocalyptic anxiety over unsolvable problems. Such relief frees us, if only temporarily, to focus on matters at hand, at least the matters that concern our hands in our own respective niches and neighborhoods.

Winds of progress still breathe hope into the narrative broth in which North American steeps. They even have plenty of historical evidence to keep them blowing. After all, aren't we exceptional in our track record of responding to change? For all but the most despairing, progress will continue. It's an article of faith. At least that's what many of us believe, or at least hope.

Maybe so, maybe not.

Progress is often interrupted, misdirected and rarely proceeds in a straight line, to be sure. Two steps forward, one step back. More will be revealed. The new normal may be signaling that belief in growth-based progress needs revising.

Whether a revision is needed or not, the belief that things will improve relies to a large extent on the promise of innovating. The promise is embedded in expressions like "where there is a will there is a way" or "necessity is the mother of invention" or "if at first you don't succeed, try, try again." Only the most cynical doubt that we *will* build the bridges necessary to get us from today's ugly problems to tomorrow's elegant solutions. Why? Because we have always built the bridges and "engines of tomorrow"[1] with the entrepreneurial will and innovating capabilities of mankind, especially with American ingenuity.

Those experienced in commercial, social or technological entrepreneurship have come to realize, however, that innovating is demanding, draining and costly. It is far from a reliable method, repeatable formula or guarantee of success. Yes, it is partly manageable, and partly not. It is inherently improvisational in process and uncertain in outcome. Yet, despite all that, innovating remains the beast that will carry the burden of hope for progress on its shoulders. A better tomorrow banks on the future inspiration, inventiveness and innovating capabilities of the clever, entrepreneurial and determined. Whether our future is clouded with foreboding threats or basking in the clear blue skies of unlimited potential, progress will continue. Besides, what is the alternative?

If there are reasons enough to continue to believe in this master engine of progress then it may be worth taking a closer look at what percentage of innovating efforts are directed where, by whom and for whom. Are they even directed to begin with, or are we really leaving it up to the invisible hand of the market? For example, do we really want all that engineering and creative talent focused on developing another app? Do we really need another digital advertising platform? Is too much investment chasing after what is possible in virtual worlds more than what is needed in the real world? Are investments in greater consumer convenience really more important than investments in what minimizes ecological footprints, ensures wider accessibility to clean water, secures basic sanitization for increasingly concentrated populations, or recovers usable energy from waste streams? Are innovations aimed at gaining competitive advantage really more deserving than innovations in the health of local communities, the redress of economic inequalities or the alleviation of systemic poverty?

Perhaps history will reveal that the current intensity of innovation activity in virtual domains will prove necessary preparations for successor innovations in physical reality, where tangible benefits come to flesh and blood. Time will tell. However, it is reasonable to posit that too much

---

1. Bouderi, *Engines of Tomorrow*, 15–25.

innovating today is undirected or misdirected, except by the invisible, anxious and greedy hands of markets obsessed with satisfying individual consumer "needs," securing an elusive sustainable competitive advantage, or seeking some kind of meaningful differentiation. What if our innovating capability was otherwise directed, perhaps by the invisible hand of the Other to care for the common good, to steward the one creation we all share and to secure a just and lasting peace between people?

What if we were able to redirect even a small percentage of our creative, inventive and innovating capability toward the needs and challenges of the common good more than consumers' convenience? What if we were to deploy some of that creative collaborative potential where the invisible hands of God may be working already?

Looking to economics alone for the decisive reasons to innovate has left us with quantitative incentives too impatient and inadequate to inspire the courage and willingness to face, address and solve problems beyond the reach of markets' invisible hands. Looking to the capabilities resident in science, technology, engineering and math (STEM) alone has led to amazing advances. But some of these advances are still looking for problems to solve. Looking to theology, however, in combination with economics, ecology and creative applications of STEM perspectives, just might broaden the field of view to see where the hands of the Other may already be at work, and just might lead us to more fruitful progress in advancing the interests of the common good.

If the theological community should become interested in this, it will need to step out of its comfort zone, become less interested in doctrinal disputes, and more interested in what its own language and methods can do to set the table for, and send out the invitation to, other disciplines for convening constructive dialogue about innovating. To do so, however, the theological community must first consider its own innovation theology.

What on earth does theology have to contribute? An answer in a sound bite might be that *theology can help us innovate for the common good.*

For a start, theology would view people not as consumers but as human beings, creatures of the Creator, not as unrelated competitors but as related neighbors. This shift in perspective—from consumer to human needs—will broaden the field of view and bring us closer to innovating in the company of God.

Theology would also look at the biosphere (creation) not simply as a set of resources to exploit but as a garden to till and to keep. Theology would likely be more inclined to view the economy—global, national or local—as a subset of the ecology[2] and thus point us to innovations in stewardship and sustainability based on sufficiency more than growth. Theology would also likely insist on re-laminating exchange, instrumental and intrinsic value into a more integrated, holistic view of just what value is.

Theology would also look for lasting security not based on economic growth, healthy bottom lines or negotiated deals but on righteousness, plumb lines and covenants, all inviting us to realign ourselves in love to God, to our neighbors, and even in reconciliation with our enemies. Innovating in the company of God reemploys our visible hands, redeploys the diverse equality of our gifts, and redirects us toward sustainable solutions for the commons, care for the creation we share, cohesion in the communities we inhabit, and security for the necessities common to us all.

While the qualitative vocabulary of theology differs from the quantitative semantics of economics, the difference really may just be between the prophetic purpose of the former and the predictive quests of the latter. Both vocabularies are needed along with the more precise words of science, technology, engineering and math. It may be the Word that is able to bring all these other words together.

Theology *can* make a contribution, one that economics, science and technology alone (or combined) cannot. Such a contribution may simply be in asking where God would have us participate in the new thing God is doing in our midst.[3] Do you not perceive it?

Perhaps there is something to consider here, in the company of God.

2. Daly and Cobb, *For the Common Good*, 4, 21.

3. Isa 43:19.

Preface

NOT LONG AGO I had what some might call a brainstorm. As with most storms, winds howl, rain pours and energy far exceeds visibility. Once the storm passes, the winds subside, the rain stops, and the air clears. Visibility improves.

Such was my experience with this brainstorm. When the storm passed I was left with a pesky vision. I was skeptical of my own thinking, remembering the observation of Peter Drucker that ideas born from brainstorms are the least reliable sources of innovation.[1] I was encouraged, however, realizing the vision was not an innovation, really. It was just an idea, one that wouldn't leave.

What I saw in my mind's eye were several conversational gatherings, each comprised of about a dozen people. Participants were those who don't normally talk to each other, partly because they live along parallel lines that seldom have the chance to meet, and partly because they may not know what to say to each other, how to say it, or even what questions to ask the other. Half the participants are theologically educated or educating. The other half are experienced innovators, entrepreneurs, economists and technologists, open to theological inquiry.

The gatherings were low profile, at least in my imagination; not a lot of promotion or glossy marketing brochures; just substantive conversations—lively, exploratory, engaging. Both halves of the room were having a lot of fun; serious, to be sure, but laughing a lot. Participants were having

1. Drucker, *Innovation and Entrepreneurship*, 130.

so much fun uncovering practical insights they decided to keep meeting, again and again.

Each participant was finding nourishment, encouragement, even inspiration from the others. It fed them all, intellectually and spiritually. The theologically educated found themselves delightfully engaged in a wider field of view than they had experienced before. The innovators found themselves encouraged, emboldened with deeper confidence, leaving each gathering with a greater clarity as to where innovations are needed and why. Others were intrigued, more than mildly. After a while, a common vocabulary began to emerge, not about doctrine or theology, really. More about value, hope and faith, and even, dare I say it, love and justice.

The initial conversations started in a few disparate parts of the continent, like the Silicon Valley, Route 128 outside of Boston, Chicago, Seattle and even Vancouver. They typically took place in a vacant classroom, one with a pristine whiteboard, which by the end of each conversation was totally filled with lines drawn between boxes and circles cryptically labeled. There were even a few equations. Before leaving most everyone pulled out their iPhones to capture for themselves the images left on the whiteboard.

Initial gatherings lasted for only a couple of hours. Soon, however, some stretched into the evening or took up a whole day. Regardless of the time, participants in these gatherings wanted to continue, as each conversation generated an energy and momentum all its own.

That's the vision that stayed after the storm in my brain blew through.

In the immediate aftermath of this brainstorm I thought the leftover vision a bit fanciful, like a daydream. The only problem was that this one didn't go away. It hung around for several weeks. In hindsight, its stickiness probably made some sense. From 1978 to 1982 I was an ordained Presbyterian minister, and since 1982 I have been a consulting facilitator to large commercial corporations attempting to invent and innovate. Some refer to me as an "innovation midwife."[2] Regardless of the label, I have had the rare privilege of living and working between two domains that seldom interact: theology and innovation.[3] These two parallel domains rarely touch, listen or speak to each other, at least publicly.

2. Vincent, "Innovation Midwives."

3. On the innovation side, mostly with STEM-intensive innovating efforts (STEM = Science, Technology, Engineering and Math) of commercial corporations; on the theology side, mostly in the context of a Reformed theological tradition as an active Presbyterian layperson.

The lack of interaction is not really surprising, at least from a conventional perspective. From a theological perspective, however, I sense both omission and opportunity, since both theology and innovation have much to say about responding to change, have to do with value and value creation, are ways people attempt to make sense, and shape human culture with positive or negative implications.[4]

Not knowing what to do with this pesky vision, I did what seemed like the obvious thing to do. I registered the domain name: innovationtheology.org. It didn't escape my notice that .net and .com were available also. I thought that would take care of it and I could go on to other things. Even such a small act as registering the domain name, however, seemed to make the vision stick even more. So, I gave into it, which was when I realized the vision had a gaping hole in it.

Suppose these gatherings *did* occur.[5] What on earth would those gathered talk with each other about? This primer might offer a beginning answer.

---

4. Such implications are often long-lasting on both creatures and the creation.

5. See www.innovationtheology.org for current status of these gatherings and conversations.

Acknowledgments

MAKING SENSE IS NOT a solo activity. This is particularly the case when it comes to making sense of uncharted territories, like innovation theology. In fact, it may not be possible without acknowledging that most everything we know, or think we know, we have received.

Such grace came to me from a greater cloud of witnesses than I could possibly acknowledge. However, there are a few who have been in the foreground of this effort, without whom I would still be wandering in the wilderness. Their theological curiosity and practical support proved essential.

Fortunately I have been blessed in this endeavor by several generous and thoughtful souls who gave their time, attention and devotion to early drafts. Substantive suggestions came from Anne Badanes, Barry Brown, Rebecca Buckley, Greg Gudorf, Amy Hassinger, Austin Leininger, John McIntyre, Matthew McNeil and Jennifer Whitten.

Subsequently Stuart Brown, Ron Gammill, Greg Gudorf, Marilyn McIntyre, Jack Swearengen each gave later drafts much close examination for which I am deeply grateful. Their advice has been both invaluable and encouraging.

Kathy Bairey brought the fresh, critical eyes of an editor to uncover what I could not see in making this a more readable set of essays. (What remains less readable is a function of my blindness, not Kathy's editorial skill.)

This effort would have languished in the wishful thinking of my mind and never made it onto the page without the encouragement, friendship and prodding of these souls. I am deeply grateful for each and every one.

Introduction

ORGANIZATIONS RESPOND TO CHANGE in different ways and for different reasons. Individuals do too. Certainly there are significant differences between what applies to an individual and what applies to an organization.[1] But what individuals do in response to change and what collectives do can prove instructive to each other.

Of course *responding* to change is different than *reacting* to change. Without a mindful pause in between the stimulus of change and our response we simply react. When we respond, we have a choice and make it. When we react, we also have a choice, but don't make it.[2] The following speaks to what we might do in this pause.

Possible responses to change range from *absorption*, where individuals and organizations have sufficient resources, momentum or clout to absorb change without adapting, to *defensive* responses where preservation and conservation are the main activities, to *innovation*, where conscious choices to respond to change create new value for others. In the case of a commercial enterprise, nonprofit or social service agency, innovation might include trying something truly new—a product or service. In the case of an individual, the new value created for another might involve the risk of doing something extra ordinary for the other.

---

1. Niebuhr, *Moral Man and Immoral Society*, xxii–xxiii: "Our contemporary culture fails to realize the power, extent and persistence of group egoism in human relations."

2. Ackoff, *Differences That Make a Difference*, 108.

Given the continuum of possible responses to change, why innovate at all? Cost/benefit calculus rarely adds up to anything but a clear warning *against* innovating. Why would anyone—organization or individual—take on the greater demands, uncertainties and risks that accompany innovating? Why attempt to respond to change in such a way to create new value?

Numbers are only one of many considerations. "The conviction of things unseen, the substance of things hoped for"[3] is another. This capability to believe what is not seen is an essential trait of the entrepreneur and innovator. That entrepreneurs and innovators use more of this capability is arguably what distinguishes them from the rest of us.[4] But whether a defining characteristic or not, believing plays a central role in the experience of innovating.

If theology[5] is thoughtful reflection on believing experiences, particularly where God is believed to play a role, then the experience of innovators innovating is well within what should interest theologians.

Another reason, especially now, is the sheer number of recent publications on entrepreneurship and innovation. Even a cursory survey of this abundance reveals that more than enough has been written on *how* organizations should innovate. Little, however, has been said about *where* innovations are needed and *why*. Some conversations related to where and why, however, are beginning. The economies of the United States, Europe and Japan, along with many organizations and individuals within them, continue to drift in the doldrums.[6] Corporate sails droop, weighed down with unprecedented piles of cash, either uninvested or underinvested. Even the US Defense Department—a traditional sponsor of many major innovations—is expressing worry that its defense contractors are not innovating like they used to.[7]

The doldrums have remained since the gale-force winds blew through in September 2008. Some economists suggest we are in the quiet after

---

3. Heb 11:1

4. Vincent, *Prisoners of Hope*, xi.

5. Unless otherwise stated, use of "theology" and its derivatives assumes biblical theology.

6. "Since 2008 corporate investment in America, the euro zone and Japan has fallen short of cashflow . . . making firms net savers rather than borrowers. This reflects both subdued expectations about near term sales and a more deep seated belief that, as populations age, markets will shrink and good opportunities for investment will become rare. Rising inequality may aggravate the process: the rich save more than the poor. Efforts by emerging markets to hold down their currencies and plough the resulting trade surpluses into rich-world bond markets do further harm" (Ip, "Dangers of Deflation").

7. Cameron and Barnes, "Pentagon Presses Contractors."

another storm of "creative destruction."[8] However, there remains much anxious money on the sidelines. What may be even more troubling than all the sidelined money is the absence of vision, hinting at the relevance of the biblical proverb "where there is no vision, the people perish."[9]

Looking back on the past three decades of involvement in innovating efforts convinces me that we need more compelling answers to the questions of where to innovate and why, answers beyond the parochial interests of the innovating organization. The answers I imagine reflect more purposeful innovations that reside in the making of meaning more than money, the pursuit of substantive more than superficial value, the quest to contribute more than simply be different, the fostering of righteous more than merely efficient outcomes, the creation of just more than merely commercial success, the stewardship of common more than shareholder's interests, and the kind of growth that is faithful more than acquisitive.

Typically we confine innovation and entrepreneurship to commercial and economic endeavors. Recently "social venturing" has extended innovation and entrepreneurship into noncommercial fields. Principles native to profit-making sectors are now being applied to opportunities for positive societal impact, not just financial gain. Many propose that one can do good while also doing well.

Seldom, however, do we recognize that theology might have something to contribute to the principles and practice of innovation and entrepreneurship, whether defined traditionally, extended to social spheres, or both. But when we realize that the essence of innovation and entrepreneurship is *creating new value for others* it opens the door to theological perspectives. The goal of what follows is to invite theological inquiry into the field of innovating and its management. What motivates such an invitation is both intellectual curiosity and practical utility.

Responding to change is fraught with uncertainty and fear. Fear afflicts both the powerless and powerful though in different ways. Neither is immune to the anxiety that comes with unsolicited change, especially when the response is aimed at creating new value. Such responses require courage. Theology suggests that faith and love are effective countermeasures to fear. "Perfect love drives out fear."[10]

8. Also called "Schumpeter's Gale."
9. Prov 29:28 KJV.
10. 1 John 4:18.

From my own direct experiences—periods of success punctuated by dashed expectations and failed plans, personal and professional—I have learned what others have learned before me: there is no more reliable source of encouragement than the clarity of one person expressing the account of their hope to another.

The Apostle Peter urged us to always be ready to give such an account for the hope that is within us.[11] The following is intended to catalyze the reader to clarify his or her own account and hope. From these experiences will grow, I believe, a conviction that unsought change is an envelope containing an invitation from a loving, caring God. In this envelope is not just any invitation. It is an invitation to create new value for others—in other words, to innovate.

CHARTING THE TERRITORY

Innovation theology is an uncharted territory at this time. The cartography of *innovation theology*[12] will require conversational efforts that traverse boundaries seldom crossed. Economists, serial inventors, theologians, biblical exegetes, lay leaders, entrepreneurs, intrapreneurs and those who study entrepreneurship and corporate venturing will need to talk with each other, and perhaps more importantly, *listen* to each other. Common charts will need to be forged that cross the boundaries of previously uncommon territories, mind-sets, experiences and vocabularies. However, despite such a daunting conversational challenge, results should lead to more substantive results for innovators, greater willingness to see change as purposeful not merely inevitable, and less reluctance to embrace innovation as an option. It could also prove enlivening to theology as well.

Innovation is normally viewed as a secular or purely economic phenomena, neither sacred nor spiritual. I am not sure why this is. The arc of the biblical saga moves from one divine intervention to another. It is filled with God intervening in the affairs of mankind to create new and unexpected events—possibilities that were unimagined and unimaginable

11. 1 Pet 3:15.

12. I could have called it a "theology of innovation" or even a "theology for innovation." I chose "innovation theology" because it has fewer words and is probably more a theology than a theory of innovation. It should not be confused with innovations for or in theology as that is what Reformed theology is already about.

before they happened. The interventions are many and varied. Take, for example,

- the birth of Isaac to a barren ninety-year-old mother;
- a burning bush that is not consumed in the burning;
- the parting of the Red Sea;
- David's inspired improvisation with five smooth stones;
- the surprise calling of Israel to be a suffering servant to all other nations;
- an exile and a return from exile;
- a messiah whose messianic character was not what most thought it should be;
- resurrections; and
- a dramatic conversion of a chief persecutor, Paul.

These are but a few of the more prominent ones, certainly not all of them. Could these divine interventions be called divine innovations? Many of these interventions *seem* like innovations—new embodiments of value that were thought impossible at first. Like many innovations they were unexpected. Still, it feels awkward to call them innovations.

If we prefer to keep divine interventions separate from human innovations, however, then reserving the latter as off limits to any considerations other than secular and economic still leaves a theological problem. It limits the scope and movement of God's presence and purpose. Imposing such a limit is *theo*logically difficult. It is contrary to one of the things typically included in the three-letter word "God": a divine freedom to show up wherever and whenever God chooses. "God does whatever God pleases."[13]

Given the few occurrences of the word "new" in theology's primary source, perhaps it is no surprise that innovation has been largely ignored by theology. However, if we pause and consider the entire sweep of the biblical narrative, Scriptures are chock-full of accounts of God doing remarkably new, unexpected and "disruptive" things—many of which were thought impossible before they became probable and actual. Rarely, however, is innovating considered from a theological perspective. Why should it be? What difference might such a perspective make, especially now?

13. Ps 115:3.

One is the legacy this generation is rapidly creating for the next. If God's interests have something to do with intrinsic values like lovingkindness, doing justice and walking humbly with God[14] then how are our innovations manifesting these intrinsic values, if at all? Are medical technology innovations—arguably embodiments of loving-kindness—constrained by the need for a profitable return? Is the requirement of a profitable return a form of *not* walking humbly? Are social media innovations enabling us to do justice by creating more and faster exposure of hidden injustices? Are these innovations at risk because they might not create enough profit even as advertising platforms? Or are these platforms generating too much noise? Are we concerned that innovations producing economic growth—revenue, profits and jobs—are also eroding the fabric of communities and relationships?[15]

Putting aside for the moment whether divine interventions are synonymous with divine innovations, all of the interventions in the biblical saga manifest the purpose and presence of God, regardless of how well or poorly we understand them. Many of them God accomplishes through people, sometimes as individuals and sometimes as leaders of tribes and nations.

Companies or organizations have purpose and presence as well, and people are the means through which companies accomplish those purposes. People are never far from where companies and organizations show up. As a result, I have elected to use the phrase "in the company of God" not solely as a convenient means to convey the presence and purpose of God. "In the company of God" also conveys God's apparent preference to involve people, even anonymously, to accomplish God's purposes.

"In the company of God" has some advantages. It suggests the presence and purpose of God. It implies that who we are and what we do and even who we do it with is either aligned with God's purpose or not. Likewise, being *in* the company of God implies that where we show up—literally, figuratively or virtually—is always relative to the position and presence of God. The phrase also implies that other people with whom we collaborate occupy positions relative to the presence of God as well. All of these implications are simply easier to express with the phrase "in the company of God," which is intended as a more vernacular surrogate for the kingdom of God on earth.

Theology, particularly biblical theology, has had much to say about transformation, liberation, reconciliation, redemption, and restoration for individuals especially. However, it has said little about innovation. This is

14. Mic 6:8.

15. Marglin, *Dismal Science*, ix.

not because it has little to say or contribute but more likely because it has not yet found ways to say it. Currently innovation is something confined to the next new thing, something that has to do with entrepreneurial activity or that which comes out of places like Silicon Valley—something subject to economic, technological and business perspectives, not theological ones.

I hope what follows proves to be at least a start in helping theology find a credible voice in matters related to innovation. Here's a look at what you will discover in this initial quest for a voice.

Chapter 1 ("Why Innovate? Curves, Chasms, and Crossings") challenges the prevailing assumption of economics that growth is necessary and an essential motivation for the innovator, given the risks and probabilities of failure that goes with innovating.

"Innovation, Theology, and Change" (chapter 2) addresses where theology connects with innovation and why such connections matter in the grand scheme of things. It proposes a bare minimum of theological givens and makes the case for the practical importance of bringing theology into the field of innovation, making the case that innovating needs theology to help answer where innovations are needed and why.

Innovating is always an effort in response to change. "Accepting Change" (chapter 3) examines how we think about change, how we feel about it, and what God might be up to in what is changing. It takes up the seductions of planning as it relates to change and speaks to the loss-filled challenges change presents. And "Reimagining Change: From Wound to Invitation" (chapter 4) makes the case that change may be an envelope through which God invites us to respond.

"Making Sense of Change" (chapter 5) recognizes how both theology and innovation are inextricably engaged in sense-making, and that making sense of change makes more sense (sorry) with God's help.

"Make Meaning *Before* Money" (chapter 6) suggests what theological inquiry can offer, perhaps better than any other field of inquiry, to innovators: a recombination of the delaminated layers of value—transactional, instrumental and intrinsic. A "re-lamination" will likely be necessary if we are going to innovate in the company of God.

"The Company of God" (chapter 7) looks at what it means to innovate in the company of God, what the company of God is (and is not) and how it is different from other companies.

Some may think I have gone off the deep end in proposing such a field as innovation theology. There may be an element of truth in this assessment.

However, the simple combination of these two words point to essential yet unexplored realities. God is not only present and at work in changes occurring around us (not just within us). God is at work in our responses to change as well, including those responses that aim to create new value for others.

Certainly not all change expresses the purposes of God. Some changes may express the opposite. Likewise, not all responses to change are aligned with the purposes of God. Some are the opposite. And indeed, not all responses to change are aimed at creating new value. However, those that succeed carry disproportionate influence on our lives and culture, for good or for ill. When they fail or are misdirected they waste an inordinate amount of energy, time and resources. As such, innovating is particularly worthy of theological consideration given the potential for contribution or waste.

Despite all the recent talk about entrepreneurship and innovation, substantive innovating has been declining for years.[16] Reasons for this are many, varied and worrisome. Might theology—that which helps us more articulately account for the hope that is within us—have an encouraging contribution to make, especially now? Continuing to look to economics—nicknamed by many the "dismal science"—may not be the best choice as a source of encouragement. Responses that broaden the field of view and invest in what's valuable to others might be better.

In short, the underlying premise of what follows is this: that God is engaged in change and that how we respond to change reflects our resistance to, or alignment with, God. Discernment is required, to be sure.[17] But to not ask whether our responses are more opposed or aligned with God's purpose and presence in change is to keep doing the same thing and expecting different results. Einstein equated this with insanity.

Rarely will our responses to change line up with God's will, precisely. To assume so reflects a lack of requisite humility at the very least. Neither does resistance to change itself necessarily represent a resistance to God's will. It could be the opposite. Nor are change and God's intentions synonymous. However, if we reframe change as an invitation from God, then to respond with love and faithfulness may represent the first steps in creating new value for others. Innovation theology should help us recognize what those first, and next steps, are.

16. Wladawsky-Berger, "Some Advice."

17. Such discernment is best done in an explicit process with others in the context of a faith community.

1

Why Innovate?

Curves, Chasms, and Crossings

CATCHING A GROWTH WAVE appears to be the prime reason to innovate. As a motivation this limits where we choose to innovate, why, and for whom.

Like surfers watching for the perfect wave, entrepreneurs search for waves with steep curves of ascending growth. Seeking the exhilaration from the powerful surge underneath, the wave's lift demands alert readiness and balance to extend the ride. This experience is not unlike what my daughter surely felt when at three years old she would implore me to keep tossing her up in the air only to catch her: "Again, again, again," she begged. Of course, I would indulge her as long as my aging and out-of-shape body could stand it.

The adoption curve is that wave so many entrepreneurial-minded seek. Popularized by Everett Rogers in the early 1960s, Rogers divided his bell-shaped curve into phases through which innovations pass from novelty to normality. Rogers named each phase by the type of adopter: "innovators," then "early adopters," then "early and late majorities." The majorities represent the steepest, fattest and most sought-after parts of the curve. But nearly thirty years after Rogers's first description, Geoffrey Moore observed a break in the wave. The continuity Rogers proposed actually hid a chasm between the early adopters and the early majority.[1]

Turns out, the adoption curve is really not all that continuous. Moore's chasm creates a frustrating challenge for innovators. Getting to the steep

1. Moore, *Crossing the Chasm*, 24.

part of the adoption curve requires a demanding crossing. Moore observed that, at least with technology-intensive innovations, there is a great gulf between early adopters and the early majority, a chasm that many never cross. The illusion of continuity tempts innovators. Surprised by the chasm they end up swallowed up in the midst of the sea, not unlike Pharaoh's chariots, wondering what happened to all that growth they anticipated. The success innovators experience *before* the chasm easily seduces them into imagining that even larger success, bigger markets and more rapid growth are just a matter of time.

The market on the other side of the chasm is actually comprised of risk-averse pragmatists, unlike the more visionary and risk-tolerant early adopters. There is a big difference between the early-but-few visionaries and the later-but-many pragmatists. The former set the trends and the latter follow them, and there is a chasm between the two.[2] Such a chasm cannot be crossed without a focused marketing effort, single-mindedly targeted to a "beachhead," from where an invasion of the larger market can be launched. Moore's theory is still ravenously consumed by hordes of technology marketers.

Less famously James Utterback offered another wave theory of how innovations progress and find adoption.[3] Utterback's two-wave theory suggests what surfers know: waves come in pairs or sets. First there is a wave of product innovation. When cresting, it's followed by a second wave of process innovation. Once product effectiveness is demonstrated then process efficiency becomes what makes the difference. When the adopting marketplace declares what it likes, the "dominant design" sets in. At this point innovators must turn their attention to what makes for efficient production conforming to the "dominant design." Utterback's gap between the two waves may not be as dramatic as Moore's chasm, but a crossing from one wave to the next is still required.

Growth curves figure prominently in many other theories of innovation, like Richard Foster's early S-curve theory[4] and Clayton Christensen's popular disruptive technology theory.[5] Despite the persuasiveness of these

2. The irony of tracking trends to spot innovation opportunities is that once trends have become apparent, the window of opportunity for innovating may have already closed. Anticipating the convergence or intersection of trends, however, can help in the identification of entrepreneurial opportunities.

3. Utterback, *Mastering the Dynamics of Innovation*, xvii.

4. Foster, *Innovation*, 89–111.

5. Christensen and Raynor, *Innovator's Solution*, 32–39.

theories, all track quantitative curves of units offered or products sold, the number of attempts tried, the number of competitors engaged and of course the holiest of holy grails, growth of the market. Few of them attend to the *value* of the innovation.[6]

Diffusion theory is only part of the innovation story, more interesting to marketers perhaps than innovators themselves. In the classic theory, Rogers calls innovators the first to use the innovation. The designation can be confusing and has even led some to conflate the diffusion of innovations with innovating itself.

Rather than leaving the subject to economic analysis alone, a theological inquiry will look at growth curves, chasms and their crossings a bit differently. Such inquiry just might relieve innovators from the tyranny of growth as the only reason to innovate. The following aims to do just that.

The year was 1986. My boss, Bill Wilson, had just returned from a meeting with his boss, Eugene Peterson. Peterson was at that time the executive vice president of engineering at Kimberly-Clark Corporation. The meeting between the two was intended, we hoped, to clarify our group's charter. "Exploratory Projects" was the name Peterson had given our staff group. This name afforded us plenty of freedom, which of course, we wanted to keep. But the name left us lacking clarity of purpose and direction, something we also wanted to have.

We had all prepared Bill for this meeting with Peterson. Just a few months before, Richard Foster had published his S-curve theory. Foster suggested innovating companies need to know not only what curve to get on, but also when to get on, and off, it. An innovator can be too early and can hang around for too long after the growth has peaked. We all thought it made a lot of sense.

Foster's theory exemplified what our group's purpose should be. At least that's what we thought. *We* should be the group in Kimberly-Clark to identify the curves. These curves would provide targets for the corporation's innovation ambitions. We had armed Bill with all sorts of examples from Kimberly-Clark's own innovating experience with innovations like Kleenex®, Kotex®, Huggies®, and even the one at that time, Depends®.

Bill returned from his meeting with Peterson and the expression on his face wasn't giving us any clues as to how the meeting went. However, we didn't have to wait long to find out. In typical fashion, Bill called us all into the conference room and revealed to us Peterson's reaction.

---

6. Except as can be inferred by the quantitative growth or incline of the curve.

His response threw us another curve. Anticipating our surprise, Bill reassured us that he had walked a quiet-but-attentive Peterson through all the key points of Foster's theory. Peterson was patient and attentive, and then gave the following response:

"This S-curve is all well and good, Bill. And it even makes a lot of sense. However, what I want to know is what's over here? What's going on there?" Bill, repeating where Peterson had pointed, put his finger on the blank space to the left of the S-curve, *off* the curve.

At first none of us understood what Peterson was talking about. We had no idea what he intended by pointing to the empty space on the chart to the left of the curve. Then Bill said to us, with the confidence of someone who had complete clarity regarding what Peterson meant: "That's where we need to look for the next innovation."

Peterson had convinced Bill that while growth curves are inherently attractive, there may be other reasons to innovate, other places to look for opportunity than those that elicit the largely imaginary and highly speculative prognostications of growth. The seed had been planted, a seed that there may be something other than growth worth paying attention to regarding where to innovate and why. About this "something other" an innovation theology has much to offer.

Growth curves are inherently limited and limiting, whether shaped like a bell or an S. These curves measure volume not value; more not better. Curves track growth, whether steep or flat. Growth curves are available only to hindsight and typically measure transactions, units sold and numbers of adopters. Such curves record popularity rather than value or quality. To be fair, value is often inferred when a curve of growth appears. But inferences are indirect at best.

Despite these limitations, however, the standard measure of success for innovating today is growth. The steeper the growth curve the more successful the innovation. These growth curves are not limited to commercial realms. Philanthropic foundations seek large-scale impacts, predicated on growth. In fact, the measure of success for an innovation—social or commercial—is whether growth is the consequence and to what degree. Return on investment is too often innovation's only metric.

But is this the only reason to innovate? Must exponential growth be the only answer to the questions of where to innovate, why and for whom?

Basic adoption theory has stood the test of time ever since Rogers first proposed it. Because it is descriptive of the delays and dynamics affecting how innovations find acceptance and spread, adoption theory offers prescriptive utility and predictive value to investors, marketers and innovators alike. However, adoption theory, along with the analysis of most economists, is predicated on the assumption that growth is always possible and always good. Theology might offer a different perspective and alternate reasons to innovate.

THE PROBLEM WITH GROWTH CURVES

First there is a problem with what comes to mind when we think of growth. It is typically extensive, quantitative or volumetric. We call it simply "more." When growth-as-more is pushed to the extreme it becomes excessive, which is aesthetically ugly, distasteful, even gross. When excessive, growth becomes exploitation, what Scripture so often calls iniquity. None other than Adam Smith might have suggested as much when he observed, "In the proportion or disproportion which the affection seems to bear to the cause . . . consists the proprietary or impropriety, the decency or ungracefulness, of the consequent action."[7]

So much for extreme or excessive growth; what of *less* excessive growth, perhaps at a more modest rate, one that does not immediately evoke an aesthetic revulsion? Even more modest rates growth, however, are viewed as having an *extensive* rather than *intensive* character. Extensive growth spreads out, broad and wide. Intensive growth, on the other hand, deepens, penetrates, and develops.

While theology's primary source (Scripture) employs both connotations for growth, theology is likely more interested in intensive than extensive growth. Isaiah speaks of this intensive understanding of growth when he expects the surviving remnant of the house of Judah "shall take root downward and bear fruit upward."[8] Such intensive growth is not confined to agricultural domains. The Apostle Paul points to this when he reflected on his own efforts, reminding the Corinthians, "I planted, Apollos watered, but God gave the growth."[9] Innovation theology will likely carry this bias for intensive more than extensive growth. It will also likely view growth as anything but a panacea.

---

7. Smith, *Theory of Moral Sentiments*, 24.
8. Isa 37:30–31.
9. 1 Cor 3:6.

Take a look at what Jesus said to one who came to him for a bit of arbitrage. He asked Jesus to tell his brother to divide their inheritance between them. Jesus replied,

> "Take care! Be on your guard against all kinds of greed; for one's life does not consist in the abundance of possessions." Then he told them a parable: "The land of a rich man produced abundantly." And he thought to himself, 'What should I do, for I have no place to store my crops?' Then he said, 'I will do this: I will pull down my barns and build larger ones, and there I will store all my grain and my goods. And I will say to my soul, Soul, you have ample goods laid up for many years; relax, eat, drink, be merry.' But God said to him, 'You fool! This very night your life is being demanded of you. And the things you have prepared, whose will they be?' So it is with those who store up treasures for themselves but are not rich towards God."[10]

To be fair this parable speaks to the *results* of growth, not of growth *per se*, though it does put us on the alert. Elsewhere Jesus speaks directly to the nature of growth itself.

> The kingdom of God is as if someone would scatter seed on the ground, and would sleep and rise night and day, and the seed would sprout and grow, *he does not know how*. The earth produces of itself, first the stalk, then the head, then the full grain in the head. But when the grain is ripe, at once he goes in with his sickle, because the harvest has come.[11]

For Jesus growth is always a gift given, not an achievement earned. And despite all our microbiological and genetic understanding, we still do not fully know how. This growth is beyond the competence, capability or capacity of humankind. This was likely established from the get-go, when "out of the ground the Lord God made to grow every tree that is pleasant to the sight and good for food" including the tree of life and the tree of the knowledge of good and evil.[12] And according to Ezekiel,

> All the trees of the field shall know that I am the Lord.
> I bring low the high tree, I make high the low tree;

---

10. Luke 12:13–21.

11. Mark 4:26–29.

12. Gen 2:9.

I dry up the green tree and make the dry tree flourish.[13]

God even reminds a recalcitrant Jonah, "You pity the plant, for which you did not labor, nor did you make it grow."[14] Planting, tilling, keeping, and harvesting are our responsibilities, not growth.

Had Jesus been a part of an industrial or digital age rather than an agricultural one, would his parables have taken on a different shape? Perhaps. We may never know. But whatever the more modern equivalent, I suspect that the growth that comes from the literal or figurative seeds we plant will remain God's to give and not ours to achieve.

The problem with growth is not growth's problem. It is our misattribution of credit for who is responsible for the growth. Believing growth is our doing or the result of our efforts alone is something an innovation theology might be slow to accept, if it allows it at all. Despite this, I suspect that the credit for growth will continue to be largely attributed to entrepreneurs, venture capitalists, philanthropists and those who take credit for innovators' work, or for God's work.

Besides, growth may or may not reflect alignment with God's purposes. We are perhaps all too quick to assume that growth is a sign of God's grace, reflective of God's blessings and validation. Extensive growth is based on more; bigger is better. Never mind that in so many areas we do not really need any more. Greatness is not bigness. Quality and character of content, not volume, is what constitutes greatness. In fact, sufficiency and sustainability are becoming the new criteria for innovation instead of growth.

The metrics of the company of God do not likely reside in volumes so much as in the lasting value, character and content of living with and for others. Either we are calculating a financial return on investment or we are clarifying what is the right thing to do. When calculating the ROI replaces doing the right thing, we allow economic, if not purely financial considerations, to preempt considerations of innovating for the common good, and the good of the commons.

Surely, it is our job to till and keep the land; our job to plant the seeds, attend to the kind of soil in which to plant them, and even to cultivate the conditions we believe conducive to sustainable growth. But this kind of growth is not the achievement of human effort. It is the result of the grace of God. Theology's perspective on growth takes it to be more of a grace given

13. Ezek 17:24.
14. Jonah 4:10.

than an accomplishment achieved. Jesus used only timeless parables of organic growth in which the growth was not an achievement of mankind. It was a gift of God.

THE URGENT PROBLEM

Any theological critique of the place growth occupies in motivating innovation efforts would be remiss if the work of Herman Daly and John Cobb were not considered. Herman Daly, an economist, and John Cobb, a theologian, collaborated in the 1980s and produced a seminal work entitled *For the Common Good*. That a credentialed economist teamed up with an equally credentialed theologian to reexamine what the majority of neoclassical economists refuse to look at, even still today, is itself worth noting. But their provisional conclusions are even more noteworthy still.

At the risk of over-simplifying their description of the urgent problem, Daly and Cobb make two basic points: first, that the global economy is a subset of the global ecology, and second, that the current growth rate of the global economy (never mind the desired growth rate), far exceeds both the source and absorptive capacities of the global ecology. Put in more theological language, God's creation and God's creatures (including human beings) are headed for a collision, the effects of which we are beginning to see in what Paul Gilding refers to prophetically as the "great disruption."[15]

> In their last chapter, Daly and Cobb propose a theological basis to guide prescriptive solutions, away from the conventional wisdom of economics, largely because with economists no real argument needs to be given for devoting oneself ultimately to the promotion of productivity and growth. No recitation of the horrors that this commitment has inflicted upon human beings, not to speak of the other creatures, no explanation that the physical conditions that made growth possible in the past are rapidly disappearing, no clarification of how human welfare can be met in other ways—none of this has yet sufficed to shake the conviction so deeply rooted in the discipline that growth is both the supreme end and the supreme means for achieving the end. Precisely by limiting the horizons of inquiry one can attain to this state of mind. The rest, economists often think, is "theology," and hence not worthy of their time.[16]

15. Gilding, *Great Disruption*.
16. Daly and Cobb, *For the Common Good*, 402.

Instead, Daly and Cobb turn directly to that theological orientation for the foundation of prescriptive solutions, even economic ones, based on four points, saying in essence that theology

- provides a check against the idolatry of growth;

- takes a point of view that necessarily transcends one's own individual interests;

- emphasizes believing which engenders commitment, something we are obviously going to need in any solution; and

- provides a necessary orientation and understanding of the future (i.e., hope as distinct from the "dismal science" of economics alone).[17]

Hence the urgent need to focus on innovations for the common good where the motivation for innovating becomes about sufficiency rather than more, about sustainability rather than size, about substance rather than convenience, about shared rather than individual benefit.

Citing the biblical prophetic tradition, Daly and Cobb observe that

> in the Bible the immediacy of God frees people *from* absolute worldly loyalties in order to bring about justice and righteousness *within* the world. The unity of love of God and love of neighbor are affirmed unequivocally. Indeed, the way to serve God truly is to serve the neighbor. What one does to the neighbor, especially the lowly neighbor, one does to God.[18]

Though Daly and Cobb focus their examination on the fallacies of growth at the macro level of global economics and ecology, their theological inquiry has implications for more local levels of business and nonprofits and the lust for growth that often manifests there.

Measurable to be sure, extensive growth is an outcome, not a purpose. Extensive growth attracts attention, but it is a poor substitute for one's sole intention. The purpose of a business[19] is to create (by means of an innovation) and serve a customer.[20] Growth is a possible outcome of serving many customers who become, *de facto*, aggregated into a market. A market is not a customer but an aggregation of many customers with similar needs.

---

17. Ibid., 401–4, with apologies to Daly and Cobb for any errors from over-simplification on my part.

18. Ibid., 392.

19. And by extension, the purpose of any organization.

20. Drucker, *Management*, 61.

Each customer, however, and the value sought by that customer remain, to a greater and lesser extent, defined by their respective and individual contexts. When growth becomes the purpose, then the business takes its eyes off the customer and attends to the market. This is the point at which the interests of the business begin to supersede the interests of the customer. When this happens, the purpose of the business has begun to drift. When this growth becomes the sole purpose of a business it becomes an idol, at least in the context of the business's entrepreneurial vocation to create and serve a customer.

When growth-as-more is pushed to the extreme it becomes excessive, exploitative, iniquitous and abhorrent. But when growth-as-better is pushed to extremes we call it excellence; those who exude excellence, we call virtuosos. Growth is simply too limited and gross a reason and measure for innovating.

If not growth, then what? What could motivate investors, innovators and entrepreneurs to risk crossings (innovations)? One obvious place to start is to "reduce the importance of consumption as a driver of growth and replace it with an enhanced role for investment."[21] The British economist Tim Jackson, teaching at the University of Surrey (UK), also suggests that

> clearly the target of investment would also need to change. The traditional function of investment, famed around increasing labor productivity, is likely to diminish in importance. Innovation will still be vital, but it will need to be targeted more carefully towards sustainability goals. Specifically, investments will need to focus on resource productivity, renewable energy, clean technology, green business, climate adaptation and ecosystem enhancement.[22]

Innovating in the company of God just might direct our attention to what God is already doing for the common good and especially to those in whom God consistently expresses a particular interest: the vulnerable and dispossessed (e.g., widows, orphans, immigrants and the poor). Or to express it less theologically, Jackson writes:

> The sense of common endeavor is one of the casualties of consumer society. We need to revitalize the notion of public goods; to renew our sense of public space, of pubic institutions, of common purpose; to invest money and time in shared goals, assets and infrastructures.[23]

21. Jackson, *Prosperity Without Growth*, 138.
22. Ibid.
23. Ibid., 193.

In short, theological inquiry will surely suggests that we need to innovate for the common good.

CHASMS WORTH CROSSING

Moore's chasms are really more about marketing than innovating. These chasms reflect unmet expectations of growth rates. Such chasms are considerably less substantive than the chasms between chronic problems and sustainable solutions; between the way things should be and the way things are; between the common good and an individual's self-interest; between the ideal and the real, the possible and the actual. More substantive chasms are likely ones that are crossed in the company of God.

Theological inquiry might suggest these other chasms and crossings. These are not chasms between different trajectories of growth, nor crossings focused merely on those who are waiting on the other side. Rather, they are chasms between self-interests and God's interests, and crossings that *carry* others from the bondage of self-centered fear to the freedom of trusting in One for whom all things are possible.

The only explicit reference to a chasm in Scripture is embedded in a parable of Jesus recorded in the Gospel of Luke.[24] It is the story of a nameless rich man and a poor man named Lazarus. Both die but end up in entirely different places. Angels carry Lazarus off to reside in the bosom of Abraham, while the rich man is unceremoniously buried and finds himself tormented in hell. The rich man looks up and sees Lazarus, far off. In anguish the rich one calls out to Father Abraham pleading for mercy. "Send Lazarus to dip the end of his finger in water and cool my tongue." But Abraham refuses, saying, "Remember that you in your lifetime received your good things, and Lazarus in like manner evil things, but now he is comforted here, and you are in agony."

And then, as if stepping aside to observe the moral reality that preceded the fate of these two souls, Abraham says, "Besides all this, between you and us a great chasm has been fixed, so that those who might want to pass from here to you cannot do so, and no one can cross from there to us."

Now this is a real chasm—an impassable, impossible, unbridgeable divide. There is no connection, no communication, no passage possible across this chasm, either one way or the other. This chasm has been fixed, or so it seems.

24. Luke 16:19–31.

But the parable doesn't stop there. It goes on through three rounds of failed bargaining by the rich man.[25] In the first round Abraham reminds the rich man that the chasm is fixed and impassable. Since no crossing is possible, the rich man then asks Abraham to send Lazarus to the rich man's father. The rich man assumes his father (presumably also dead) is on Lazarus' side of the chasm. Might his father be in a position to warn his other sons so as to avoid the fate that befell the rich man? But here Abraham demurs, "They have Moses and the prophets; let them hear them." So much for the second round.

Undaunted, the rich one tries a third time pleading, "If someone goes to them from the dead, they will repent." Surely Abraham could have responded with a little compassion. But Abraham says, "If they do not hear Moses and the prophets, neither will they be convinced if someone should rise from the dead."

This chasm is perhaps the greatest chasm of all: the chasm between the living and the dead. Theology might claim that this chasm *has been* crossed, and indeed, is still being crossed; a crossing that requires faith, obedience and the company of God, to be sure. But a chasm that Abraham, at least, regards as similar to the chasm crossed by Moses that gave birth to the "old" covenant, indeed, gave birth to the liberated people of Israel, no longer enslaved to Pharaoh's bondage.

According to the Gospel of Luke, Jesus' parable makes explicit what is common between the new chasm to be crossed and the old chasm Moses crossed with the people of Israel.

The chasm between "dead" and "living" is layered with meaning and promise in the company of God. This chasm points to where innovations are truly needed and why, and indeed, for whom. To put it simply, what theology can bring that economics cannot is the call to innovate where there is little if any hope, for people who have little if any hope. This is ultimately where the company of God invites us to create new value for others.

Innovating in the company of God is about crossing chasms between different need states not between different growth rates. Chasms of economic inequalities, social asymmetries, racial prejudices, and environmental exploitations are where innovations (crossings) are needed. We need to redeploy our innovating time, attention and devotion to economic sufficiency instead of unbridled growth, to environmental sustainability instead

---

25. Is this bargaining a core competence of the rich, or merely a stage in his grieving process?

of ecological extractions, to equitable security instead of human exploitation, and to societal solvency instead of precarious, unstable peace.

If theology has anything significant to say to innovating efforts, has anything to contribute to clarifying where innovations are needed, why and for whom, then theology is likely to ask innovators whether what they are doing (why and for whom) has anything to do with the will and purposes of a living and loving God. Should the answer be less than satisfying then a follow-on question might be whether the innovating effort can be realigned with the company of God? If this follow-on question is answered with the question "What is the will of God?" an answer can always be found in who the other is for whom new value is created: those whom Jesus referred to as the "lost sheep" in contrast to the ninety-nine.[26] These "sheep" are not "consumers," much less a market. They are people, who have lost their way, have unmet needs (vs. wants), needs that may be rather basic more than "virtual" or digital. Innovating in the company of God is surely directed toward these, the least of these.

All this might challenge the conventional return on investment (ROI) logic. "Just so," Jesus says, "I tell you, there will be more joy in heaven over one sinner who repents than over ninety-nine righteous people who need no repentance."[27] Again, "Just so, I tell you, there is joy in the presence of the angels of God over one sinner who repents."[28] Clearly ROI in the company of God is calculated upon a different basis.

We have an abundance of educated talent, credentialed engineers, experienced computer coders, capable material and life scientists and even skilled architects and designers in the "softer" disciplines. What if even a small percentage of them were directed toward challenges facing the care of creation, the correction and prevention of social injustice and the sustainable reconciliation of economic inequities?

Some are starting to point in this direction. One is Jeff Hammerbacher, former manger of the Facebook Data Team and founder of Cloudera, who is often quoted as saying, "The best minds of my generation are thinking about how to make people click ads. That sucks."[29]

Too many of our brightest minds are directed toward designing additional advertising platforms creating more entertainment "content" or

26. Luke 15:3–7.
27. Luke 15:7.
28. Luke 15:10.
29. Mele, *End of Big*, 25.

improving convenience instead of the care of others and creation itself. If we were innovating in the company of God, we would be more apt to create new value for others that is common, shared and of redemptive and reconciling purpose. Innovations in the company of God will likely be aimed more at what benefits the common good and speak more to our shared physical, economic and perhaps even emotional security. These innovations may at first appear to be islands of care and mutual interdependence in oceans of indifference and seas of self-reliance. Too much of our innovating chases ROI. The returns are typically measured by scale (i.e., large and/or wide, at least relative to the money or effort invested). In commercial contexts these returns are monetized by profit or shareholder value.

Our current innovating efforts could use a little theology, don't you think? Jesus didn't appear to be particularly enamored with ROI, shareholder value or profit for that matter, though he didn't disallow it either. He was, however, more interested in the one out of ninety-nine lost sheep, or the one out of ten lost coins.[30]

Don't get me wrong. Deploying theological inquiry to judge whether an innovation or related technology is good or bad is overreaching. Doing so would confuse theology with ethics. Nor is the interest here to declare all innovations and their respective technologies morally neutral. The intent, rather, is to realize and actualize the idea that theology can raise the question of purpose more quickly, holistically and compellingly than any other field of inquiry. Sooner or later theology will ask what is the purpose, will or intent of God and if the innovation effort is even remotely aligned with that purpose. Merely asking this question remains a prophetic but hopeful reminder that in the company of God purpose, meaning, and reconciliation are possible.

CROSSINGS

Experienced practitioners of innovation have long recognized that innovating involves crossing boundaries. Do a key word search with "crossing boundaries and innovation" and marvel at the number of citations (2.8 million when I tried it). Cross-functional, cross-disciplinary and diverse perspectives are widely recognized as essential to any credible innovating effort.

Successful innovating happens "at the seams" where traditional boundaries are crossed—conceptual, academic and even geographic and cultural.

30. Luke 15:7, 10.

Innovations cross boundaries between what was previously believed to be impossible, improbable or infeasible. Frans Johansson has gone so far as to describe two general types of boundary-crossings manifest in most innovations.[31] One he calls *directional*, where the boundaries crossed reside within a particular field. The other he calls *intersectional*, where the boundaries crossed reside between different fields. In either case, boundaries are crossed.

How the crossing is made may be as significant as that a crossing is required. How the crossing is made will also depend on the nature of the chasm crossed.

Moore's crossing strategy, appropriate for chasms of different growth rates, is to concentrate time, attention and resources on a single beachhead. Borrowing from the success of the D-day invasion of Normandy, Moore's crossings assume chasms like the English Channel, where the way across is by buoyantly traversing the surface of the waters in more or less a straight line. The crossing trajectory is up and over.

The crossings innovation theology likely has in mind will be significantly different, primarily because the chasms in which the company of God is more interested are different—more likely about what separates us from substantive meaning, sustainable value, sufficient satisfactions and shared commons. Crossings of these chasms require a different route altogether.

Since these chasms are less about gaps in growth rates and more about what separates people from becoming who God intended them to be, the crossings carry people rather than marketing messages. These crossings are not about focused marketing strategies, but about reconciling differences and creating a sustainable bridge for others to cross, and keep crossing. The crossings are not likely to be up and over, but down and then up; death before resurrection, a sacrifice of self-interest for the interest of others.[32] A seed must sacrifice itself and die before life and intensive growth can come from it.

This may not be simply an interesting theological principle. It may have practical relevance for innovating. Otto Scharmer, Peter Senge and others have made the case for what they call the "social technology of *presencing*."[33] It reflects this down-and-then-up crossing strategy. It resonates with what leaders and innovators have actually experienced in their innovating efforts. "*Presencing* is a blending of the words 'presence' and 'sensing.' It means to

31. Johansson, *Medici Effect*, 17–20.

32. Paul called this the wisdom of God and observed that the world regards it as "foolishness" (1 Cor 1:21–25; 3:19).

33. Senge et al., *Presence*, 218–21.

sense, tune in, and act from one's highest future potential—the future that depends on us to bring it into being."[34] Senge observes that

> change efforts usually focus on making changes in "them" or in "the system" or on "implementing" a predetermined "change process," or in fixing some other externalized object—rarely on how "I" and "we" must change in order to allow the larger system to change.[35]

When innovating as a response to change requires the innovators themselves to change, we are now speaking a language familiar to theology, especially in its prophetic sources. There it is called repentance, a turning away from something old that results in a turning toward something new.

While current thinkers are rediscovering this way of crossing chasms, theology might relook at its own primary crossing in a new light. The ancient crossing I have in mind is the crossing of the Red Sea, the climax of the Exodus story.

Given how often we assume familiarity with the Exodus story, it is worth a pause to look at the actual canonical account. Here's the narrative as it is represented in the book of Exodus:

> The Lord said to Moses, "Why do you cry out to me? Tell the Israelites to go forward. But you lift up your staff, and stretch out your hand over the sea and divide it, that the Israelites may go into the sea on dry ground.
>
> "Then I will harden the hearts of the Egyptians so that they will go in after them; and so I will gain glory for myself over Pharaoh and all his army, his chariots, and his chariot drivers. And the Egyptians shall know that I am the Lord, when I have gained glory for myself over Pharaoh, his chariots, and his chariot drivers."
>
> The angel of God who was going before the Israelite army moved and went behind them; and the pillar of cloud moved from in front of them and took its place behind them. It came between the army of Egypt and the army of Israel. And so the cloud was there with the darkness, and it lit up the night; one did not come near the other all night.
>
> Then Moses stretched out his hand over the sea. The Lord drove the sea back by a strong east wind all night, and turned the sea into dry land; and the waters were divided. The Israelites went into the sea on dry ground, the waters forming a wall for them on their right and on their left. The Egyptians pursued, and went into

34. Scharmer, *Theory U*, 8.
35. Ibid., xiv.

the sea after them, all of Pharaoh's horses, chariots, and chariot drivers. At the morning watch the Lord in the pillar of fire and cloud looked down upon the Egyptian army, and threw the Egyptian army into panic. He clogged their chariot wheels so that they turned with difficulty. The Egyptians said, "Let us flee from the Israelites, for the Lord is fighting for them against Egypt."

Then the Lord said to Moses, "Stretch out your hand over the sea, so that the water may come back upon the Egyptians, upon their chariots and chariot drivers." So Moses stretched out his hand over the sea, and at dawn the sea returned to its normal depth. As the Egyptians fled before it, the Lord tossed the Egyptians into the sea.

The waters returned and covered the chariots and the chariot drivers, the entire army of Pharaoh that had followed them into the sea; not one of them remained. But the Israelites walked on dry ground through the sea, the waters forming a wall for them on their right and on their left.[36]

There is more than enough related to innovation theology in this crossing story to keep a theological inquiry going for some time.[37] Most relevant to our interest in crossing chasms however, are the particulars of this crossing. There at least four that present themselves.

First, the crossing is unambiguously an act of God. This act of God is an unanticipated and miraculous intervention, one that certainly challenges common notions of historicity, empiricism and even believability. But if God is the One for whom all things are possible,[38] then such uncertainties fade into the shadows cast by the light of this story's unambiguous attribution of the One who makes the crossing possible. Clearly, the not-so-hidden assumption operating here is that God is both interested and engaged, not the disinterested or disengaged Watchmaker who has designed and made the clock, wound it up, and set it aside to run its course. "The Lord drove the sea back." "He [the Lord] clogged their chariot wheels." "The Lord tossed the Egyptians into the sea." This was not some off-handed, inadvertent effect of a disinterested divine being.

36. Exod 14:15–22.

37. Such as the "hardening of Pharaoh's heart" as an apt expression for the resistance that is a part of most every innovating story, or the protective shelter ("pillar of cloud") that repositions itself hinting at the practice of so many experienced R&D leaders who know their role is to offer "top cover" for any vulnerable innovating effort.

38. See chapter 2, especially assumption #4.

Second, God did not act alone. While clearly God is the main actor in this crossing, God assigns Moses a specific role and responsibility—to stretch out his hand over the sea, twice in fact, both before and after the crossing. Might we say the crossing is an act of God while the timing is in the hands of Moses? The crossing is a collaborative effort, not only between God and Moses. God also seems quite willing to use all means available to embody this intervention, including a "strong east wind" that blows all night long to drive the waters back and the overwhelming potential of the waters themselves to cover. Even the residual moisture of the ground "clogged their chariot wheels." God appears to prefer interventions aided and abetted by the collaboration of others—both other people and other natural elements.

Third, those making the crossing stepped forward. This could be another example of God not acting alone. However, calling it out separately reminds us that God is likely to have not only a collaborative bias but a preference for inviting us to participate. While the story doesn't leave the Israelites with much of a choice, the biblical witness consistently gives us an image of God as one who invites us not only to follow but to "go forward" (not backward!), regardless of the uncertainty and seeming impossibilities that going forward may appear to present. Other examples of this include the binding of Isaac[39] or the prior promise to Sarah that even though she was well past her potential for pregnancy, she would bear a son.[40]

There are many examples of this call to step forward, especially when we are not sure. Crossings like this evoked the famous definition of faith found in Hebrews: "the substance of things hoped for, evidence of things unseen," and the rather lengthy list of examples that followed.[41] Even Albert Einstein, who crossed significant scientific chasms, alluded to this step-forward faith in the advice he wrote in a letter to his son Eduard, saying, "Life is like riding a bicycle. To keep your balance you must keep moving."[42] Crossings seem to require us to step forward ourselves, even in the company of God.

Fourth, the crossing is on dry ground. Nearly equal to the miracle of the parting of the seas is the dryness of the ground over which the Israelites crossed. The crossing was made on terra firma, offering the sure footing

39. Gen 22.
40. Gen 12, 15, 16.
41. Heb 11:1 KJV.
42. Isaacson, *Einstein*, 367.

that only dry ground can offer. They neither treaded water in the chaotic seas of ambiguity, nor were tossed about in the turbulence of uncertainty on the surface. The crossing was made on the ground and it was dry.

Innovation in the company of God may likely show up more on *dry ground* than elsewhere—innovations that are substantive more than superficial or virtual; material more than digital. While so much recent innovating effort has gone into the virtual domain, God may have a greater interest in the material domain. This possible preference, provisionally offered here, should give us all considerable pause as we consider where innovations are needed, why, and for whom. Looking to growth perpetuated by virtual realities or aided and abetted by big data, may not be as keen an interest of the company of God.

Herman Daly suggests as much in his observation that

> we have an inordinate faith in solutions by technical improvement and practically no faith in solutions by moral improvement. Growth seems to absolve us from the duty to control population and to share the earth's resources more equitably among members of the present generation and between the present and future generations.[43]

Instead of growth, sustainable development might provide a motivation for clarifying where innovations are needed, why and for whom, at least in the company of God.[44] Innovations so motivated will address sufficiency as much as efficiency and its related technologies. Such innovations may be oriented less to throughput than to stewardship, harvesting rates of renewable resources calibrated not-to-exceed regeneration rates while using nonrenewables at rates not exceeding the creation of renewable substitutes.[45] Technological innovations in these areas will be challenging enough and certainly appear more urgent, important and deserving of our technological capabilities than the quest for more convenience or more digital advertising platforms. This is what it may mean for us today to make crossings "on dry ground"; perhaps, dry *common* ground.

Innovations themselves cross chasms. In the company of God these crossings might cross not "over" but down, into and up from the chasm itself. In the company of God, these crossings (or innovations) are not merely transformations. They are transfigurations, incarnations and resurrections;

43. Daly, *Steady-State Economics*, 206–7.

44. Daly, *Beyond Growth*, 219.

45. Daly, *Steady-State Economics*, 256.

often wordless, nonverbal and empathetic forms of communicating that demonstrate more than describe meaning and value. And what these innovations communicate, if they are even modestly successful, is that the other for whom they are intended is both heard and beheld, and to some extent understood and served. There innovations may reconcile perhaps even more than they redeem, and they cross over on the dry, solid ground of non-exploitive value, value that is recognized even before it is described.

Many chasms can be crossed horizontally. Some, however, cannot be crossed without the intervention from the vertical dimension, the transcendent reality that makes the crossing possible. Such verticality either preempts or dissolves trade-offs possible only when the horizontal is considered. Like a suspension bridge, some height is required, some "looking up" (as did the rich man lifting up his eyes to see Abraham and Lazarus) not only to the other side of the chasm, but upward, to another altitude altogether.

So what? Why do curves, chasms and crossings matter at all?

CONCLUSION

The measure of success for most innovating efforts today is growth. The steeper the growth curve the more successful the innovation. Conventional economics looks to evidence of quantitative growth as the measure of success for both innovation in general and a specific innovation in particular. If an innovation is able to "cross the chasm" between early adopters and the early majority, the entrepreneur has achieved the goal—exponential growth.

In the company of God, however, success is likely defined differently. Value is not just extrinsic or only instrumental. It is also intrinsic, covenantal. In the company of God people are not only consumers but also children of God. In the company of God growth is something that goes deeper, not just broader, something that is transfiguring, not just expanding. In the company of God relationships are more important that acquisitions, life is more important than transactions, covenants are more important than contracts. While economists may be satisfied with growth as the prerequisite for a healthy economy, engineers satisfied with improvements as essential for progress, psychologists with happiness as the goal, political scientists with a just and ordered society; those with a theological sense may not be satisfied at all, unless the creation and creatures, including humankind, be more closely aligned with the will of God.

Without the benefit of theological inquiry somewhere early in choosing where to innovate, why and for whom, we will likely be left with growth as the sole measure of success. Innovating with at least some theological inquiry, however, just might give us sustainability as an alternate measure. In fact, innovating with some theological consideration just might reframe success as a part of a longer-term succession rather than an unsustainable episode of exponential growth, flattening as it inevitably does when the S-curve peaks.

A biblical theology of innovating might look for a different kind of evidence as the measure of success, not based on quantitative growth but qualitative development. This means that regardless of the ensuing slope of the growth curve, there is something more important than quantitative metrics with which to gage the success of an innovation or innovator; a significant improvement in the quality of life for the innovation's beneficiary, whether an individual or a community, or a world.

Theology has some experience with curves, chasm and their crossings, though they are not confined to growth and adoption. Theology's curves have to do with deep and dark descents followed by steep ascents—curves "with wings like eagles"[46]—conversion curves of repentant reversals. Its chasms stretch wide and far, and include broken covenants, exilic separations, unbelievable demands and pride-swollen exceptionalism—chasms keeping God from mankind and mankind from God. Its crossings move from death to life, from exploitation to liberation, from man to God and God to man—crossings thought improbable if not impossible, until the One for whom all things are possible made, with and for us, one crossing after another.

In the end, however, what theology can bring to innovating is limited. It certainly cannot bring technological content to innovating. However it can bring inspired, renewed heart, mind and hands to innovators, so long as we are sincerely working in the company of God, aligned with the One who can do for us what we cannot do for ourselves, One for whom all things are possible.

46. Isa 40:31.

2

Innovation, Theology, and Change

WHAT DOES INNOVATION HAVE to do with God? What does God have to do with innovation?

"Not much" seems to be the conventional answer. After all, innovating is a human, socioeconomic or cultural phenomenon. It represents nothing more than the intersecting dynamics of technology applications and market diffusions—simply societal phenomena.

Such an answer has practical implications for both organizations and individuals. For organizations it leaves decisions on where to innovate and why captive to financial considerations more than anything else. It adds kindling to the smoldering notion that economy is more important than community.[1] In more personal contexts the exclusion of any divine interest in innovation leaves individuals with only a calculator to make trade-offs when confronted with tough choices. Why bother to invent solutions that transcend trade-offs if nothing transcendent is at stake? Why be concerned with the deeper, more intrinsic values when the extrinsic ones are "just good enough"?

If God is neither interested nor engaged in innovating then we have limited what interests God. Presuming we know the scope of God's interests is not only arrogant. Such a presumption places us above God—a theologically untenable position. When we answer "not much," we make

1. Marglin, *Dismal Science*, 1. Marglin convincingly argues that community forms a necessary societal "infrastructure" for any economy. Economic development that ignores more fundamental community values and structures undermines the very foundation the economy assumes.

an assumption about God, an assumption about innovation, and reveal the limits of our own theological imaginations. If innovation has nothing to do with God then we assume there are boundaries on God's interests and relegate innovation to be "out of bounds" for God.

On the other hand, if "something" is our answer, it implies an innovation theology of some kind, however implicit. If God *is* interested and actually *does* have something to do with innovating, then questions like where and why God is interested, and what difference God's interests make, come to the surface. Discerning the nature, character and location of this divine interest becomes both relevant and urgent.

As you might imagine, my basic premise is that God *does* have something to do with innovation and innovation something to do with God. This is a claim that is accessible through faith, and possibly through the pragmatic logic reminiscent of Pascal's wager.[2] But whether by faith, logic or wager, "something" seems a more prudent answer, and that God's interest in innovation remains regardless of whether innovators are conscious of it or not. If innovation does interest God then making innovation theology more explicit is worth doing.

In such an effort, we will need to consider where innovation theology can be located in the context of other types of theology and among other perspectives on innovation, like economics, anthropology, technology and diffusion theory, to name a few. What kind of biblical foundations provide the base for such a theology? What is the purpose or function of such a theology? Will it have its own peculiar methods? All these things and more will need to be considered as we start to construct an innovation theology.

If an innovation theology can be built, it will likely end up an applied theology—one that derives truths and principles from theology proper and applies those principles to innovating practice. Theological groundwork necessary for pouring the foundation for any innovation theology will need to consider which critical few assumptions about God are essential for such a theology and what purpose such a theology might serve.

---

2. The 17th-century French philosopher observed that all humans bet with their lives either that God exists or not, and that it is almost self-evident that it is more prudent, if not rational, to believe in God and live accordingly than the alternative. If, it turns out that God does exist and we choose not to believe it, then we are much worse off.

ASSUMPTIONS FROM THEOLOGY PROPER

Pure theology explores the existence, nature and character of God, whether based on revealed or "natural" sources. Innovation theology, on the other hand, will necessarily build upon foundation claims made about God by theology proper.

While innovation theology may share the same foundation as other applied theologies, the application space has a different focus and interest. Therefore, innovation theology will be interested in parts of theology proper more directly related to its purposes, methods and interests. *Attributes* of God are likely more essential to any innovation theology than are arguments for the existence of God. As an applied theology, God's existence is assumed, not argued. As a result, little attention is given to arguments for the existence of God here. For that plenty has been written. God's attributes, however, prove to be more influential in shaping what an innovation theology might look like.

The aphorism "everything should be made as simple as possible, but no simpler"[3] guides which of the divine attributes from theology proper to select as most relevant. I might add another criteria—those theological claims most self-evident or least controversial. I confess that by saying "self-evident" assumptions about God, I necessarily reveal my own theological bias and tradition.[4]

There are at least four "self-evident" assumptions that will likely be part of any foundation for innovation theology. These four will influence and shape what innovation theology might become and the pragmatic value it may eventually provide. The four are as follows:

> Assumption 1: God exists.
>
> Assumption 2: God is still creating.
>
> Assumption 3: God loves.
>
> Assumption 4: God is One for whom all things are possible.

Another assumption—that Jesus embodied all these assumptions[5]—could easily be added. Some might argue for a shorter list of assumptions,

3. Often attributed to Albert Einstein as heard by the American composer Roger Sessions.

4. My own theological background is Protestant in tradition, Presbyterian in denomination and Reformed in theology. Hopefully I am not stuck in these perspectives, but readily acknowledge the resulting bias of this background.

5. The implications of Christology on these assumptions and innovation theology may make a significant difference in the architecture of innovation theology and should be considered for further discussion and investigation.

modifying the way one or more of these assumptions is expressed. Still others might object that other assumptions should be included—for example, an assumption or two about Jesus Christ and his death, resurrection and ascension, or about a Trinitarian God, or about grace, atonement, etc. All of these are interesting variations that may be worth exploring.

The limited scope of my intent is to invite rather than address these possibilities. I hope theological cases will be made in the future for such inclusions, alternate expressions or combinations. My present objective in listing these four assumptions is not to defend as much as to suggest that these may be a bare minimum of the critical few theological assumptions necessary for constructing an innovation theology.

Each of these four foundational assumptions deserves some attention in order to make their relevance to innovation theology apparent.

ASSUMPTION 1:
GOD EXISTS

Arguments for the existence of God are many and varied. These arguments have garnered attention and study for thousands of years and have been based on revelation, nature, philosophy, "pure reason," pragmatic probability and phenomenology. The recent resurgence of adamant atheists has re-plowed the field of these arguments, sometimes without a lot of consideration for the breadth, depth and longevity of the "prior art." Innovation theology should not take up these arguments. That is the job of theology proper. However, innovation theology will necessarily build upon the outcomes of one or more of these arguments for the existence of God.

Obviously, any effort to construct an innovation theology would not get very far without the assumption that God exists. Whether one or more of the many arguments for the existence of God will have a material bearing on the nature and character of innovation theology, I leave to better theological minds than mine to discern. Suffice it to say for now, that any innovation theology that does not include this most basic assumption, for whatever reason, is dead in the water.

There are certain implications of the claim *God exists* that will have a bearing on innovation theology. For example, if God exists, then it follows logically, at least for some, that God is living, interested and actively engaged. Some of this is implied in the next assumption, which makes the implication of God's existence a bit more explicit than the bald statement that God exists.

ASSUMPTION 2:
GOD IS STILL CREATING

Some have conceived of God as a passive watchmaker.[6] Once God finished creating the world, having "wound it up," so to speak, God took a detached position, letting the mechanisms of creation play out.

This view, while still held by many, is not likely to provide a supportive foundation for any innovation theology. Instead, an innovation theology will likely assume a God who acts and intervenes in both the history of mankind and in the natural processes of creation. This active, even interventionist, view of God is arguably more aligned with the Old Testament witness, and certainly a central assumption behind the intervention of God in and through the pre- and post-resurrected Jesus. The Apostle Paul's bold statement that "the whole of creation has been groaning in labor pains until now"[7] suggests a Creator God who is committed and not finished. A passive, "watchmaker" kind of God is likely not going to be a working assumption of any innovation theology.

While it is theologically appropriate to acknowledge that in creation God established a natural order to things, it does not necessarily follow that once established, God stopped working, or stopped creating. "Do not remember the former things, or consider the things of old," says Isaiah.[8] "I am about to do a new thing; now it springs forth, do you not perceive it?" There is certainly some evidence, theological, scriptural and even phenomenological, to suggest that God is not finished yet.

Take a look at the first two verses of Genesis. Even *before* the first day of creation, the first verse of Scripture describes God as One who is creating. This is as much as we know about God, at least as far as Scripture tells us, thus far in the canon. Everything else we imagine about God we are importing.

"In the beginning God created . . ." is the more familiar translation. However, just as acceptable is another: "In the beginning when God began to create . . ." This translation suggests God may have started creating in the beginning but may not have ever retired from it, except for a day off at the end of each "week." Indeed, if we jump ahead to the seventh day of creation—the day that God rested "from all the work that he had done in

6. Paley, *Natural Theology*, ch. 1.

7. Rom 8:22.

8. Isa 43:18–19.

creation"[9]—we might get the impression that God was done creating. But the text doesn't quite say that. It says, rather, "God finished *the work he had done.*" This does not imply that God had no more work to do. In fact, taking a day off to rest might imply the next morning God returns back to work, creating. That God is still creating is a reasonable assumption.

Look even more closely at these first two verses in Genesis. Verse 2 says that the "earth was without form and void, and darkness covered the face of the deep, while a wind from God swept over the face of the waters." Even before there is light (God's first act of creating) there is movement. The Spirit of God (*ruah* in Hebrew means "breath" or "wind") is moving. It moves across the waters, which themselves move in reaction to the unseen stimulus. Highly susceptible to stimulus, water is rarely, if ever, still. When it is we call it "dead."

Movements vary. In the subsequent days of creation various creating movements are mentioned, including *separating* the waters above from the waters below (day 2), *gathering* the waters under the sky, and vegetation *yielding* seed and fruit (day 3), *lighting* the earth and *marking* the days, seasons and years (day 4), *bringing forth* every living creature that moves and creeps (day 5 and 6).

Thus far the only "image of God" we have at this point is of a creator: creating, living, breathing, moving. All these partial images don't stand independently from each other. Like threads in a fabric of reality that is woven together, integrated, moving, breathing and living are contiguous, successive and of one continuous flow. Even in the second creation account in Genesis[10] *before* plants or herbs or rain, God forms man from the dust of the ground and breathes into this form, specifically into the nostrils of this form, the breath of life. As a result, "the man became a living being."[11] There is a similar explicit equation of life, living, breathing (and the Spirit of God) and movement in Ezekiel's vision of the valley of the dry bones.[12]

Movement implies change, as does the coordinated acts of mind and hand we call creating. Creating, changing and moving is more the norm than most of us think.[13] Even what we most often regard as "given," like the

9. Gen 2:2.

10. Gen 2:2.4.

11. Gen 2:7.

12. Ezek 37.

13. Carr, *Henri Bergson*, 18. The philosophy of Henri Bergson examines this "fabric" is great detail. Movement is life and life is movement, suggested the French philosopher

"foundations of the earth and heavens," God can change like an article of clothing.[14] God's presence may be constant, but God's creating is constantly changing, generating, and generous. Genesis, the first book of Scripture is well named. It is hard to avoid the generative generosity of a creating God.

ASSUMPTION 3:
GOD IS LOVE[15]

This assumption could be regarded as implicit in the second assumption. However, I include it here as its own assumption for two reasons.

The first is to be explicit about the disposition of God toward God's creation, including both the earth, what lives and moves on the earth, and mankind. Love, of course, can and should be viewed as more than a disposition of God. It could be in some mysterious way an (or the) essential attribute of God's entire being. Hence, "God is love." Whether this is a disposition or an attribute of God or the essential being of God, is better left to theology proper. So much has been written about this characteristic of God that we can generally accept the widespread consensus in regards to these three words "God is love" arranged as they are.

The second reason for including this assumption may have more to do with innovation than God. Innovators, particularly successful ones, are often seduced by the admiration of others and their own success. Succumbing to this temptation leads to boasting in their own wisdom, strength, and often in their resulting wealth. In so doing, these successful role models often end up implying they have a proven and therefore replicable formula for successful innovation.

However, while their experience and success may be indisputable, replicability does not necessary follow, logically or in practice. In fact, "success is often the enemy of innovation."[16] Success can easily erode humility. When we assume "God is love," it may also be useful to remind ourselves that love is not simply an emotion or a disposition. Love also has to do with matters of justice and righteousness, even truth and reality. Love and success are two words that do not necessarily comfortably reside with each other.

Henri Bergson. Where there is no movement, there is no life.

14. Ps 102:25–27; Heb 1:10–12.

15. 1 John 4:8.

16. Said by David Chernin, former COO of Fox, at a strategy meeting I facilitated some years ago.

Whatever other theological notions people have about God, the prophet Jeremiah's way of combining steadfast love, justice and righteousness, and leading off with steadfast love—is a combination worth keeping in mind. It keeps innovators humble, implies an understanding of love as more than mere feeling, and expresses an inseparable triad of love, justice and righteousness. This triad avoids a superficial sentimentalism of mistaking love as primarily a feeling or disposition. Here's the way Jeremiah[17] puts it:

> Thus says the Lord, "Do not let the wise boast in their wisdom,
>
> do not let the mighty boast in their might,
>
> do not let the wealthy boast in their wealth;
>
> but let those who boast boast in this,
>
> that they understand and know me, that I am the Lord;
>
> I act with steadfast love, justice and righteousness in the earth,
>
> For in these things I delight," says the Lord.

ASSUMPTION 4:
GOD IS ONE FOR WHOM ALL THINGS ARE POSSIBLE[18]

Of the four, this assumption may be the most directly encouraging for innovators. As a foundation assumption it is certainly the closest to a tautology. For God all things are possible. If there were any limits on God then God would not be God. If we limit God's freedom, competence, capability or capacity by inferring that there is anything that God cannot do, we make a fundamental error in logic, or *theo*-logic. Putting any limits on God is a direct and logical contradiction. We do this more often than we may realize, particularly when we take a detached, objective and reasoned point of view of God.

Such a detached perspective requires a perch from outside the creation, "outside" of God or God's influence, or a more arrogant, "looking down upon" God. With any one of these points of view, we end up taking God's perspective—a perspective that we cannot take, by definition. Such a perspective is not only a logical contradiction. It is also practically

17. Jer 9:23–24.

18. Brueggemann, *Reality, Grief, Hope,* 157. Brueggemann highlights this way of describing God, citing Kierkegaard. Kierkegaard was not necessarily the author of this assumption, however, as we can find plenty of direct and indirect evidence of this assumption in Matt 19:26; Mark 9:23; 10:27; and Luke 18:27.

impossible. That we do it anyway, repeatedly, is one of the great sources of trouble for mankind.

If God is God, then neither you nor I are. Rather we are a *part of* God's creation and within or under the umbrella of God's perspective and care, a position that by definition we cannot get out from under even if we wanted to or think we can.

This fourth assumption is particularly pertinent to innovation theology, given that innovating has so much to do with converting what is possible into what is real. First-person accounts of innovators and third-person case studies consistently reveal the following pattern of innovating. Innovating starts with a change. The change reveals a problem or opportunity "as given."[19] This is the initial stimulus, inciting innovators to conceive of a few potential solutions and even try them out. Then, inevitably, these solutions encounter rejection and resistance, especially if the solution is new. Somewhere along the way in this process the original problem "as given" morphs into a problem "as understood." Then a more evolved and refined solution is conceived, developed and ultimately introduced. This pattern holds true whether the innovating effort is successful or not, and regardless of the context in which the innovating is done, personal or corporate, social or commercial.

Innovating requires persistence. Many regard persistence as an essential characteristic of entrepreneurs and innovators, for good reason. Innovation, if it is really innovation, will be resisted, if not at first rejected. This was expressed centuries ago by Nicolo Machiavelli's (1469–1527) in *The Prince*:

> There is nothing more difficult to carry out nor more doubtful of success, nor more dangerous to handle than to initiate a new order of things; for the reformer has enemies in all those who profit by the old order, and only lukewarm defenders in all those who would profit by the new order; this lukewarmness arising partly from the incredulity of mankind who does not truly believe in anything new until they actually have experience of it.

Machiavelli's "reformer" is our innovator. Innovating "initiates a new order," whether out of chaos or out of a more familiar context.

As a result, this fourth assumption—"that God is one for whom all things are possible"—is a potent source of encouragement and hope for

---

19. Is this "givenness" a grace embodied in purposefulness, task and vocation? Innovation theology might suggest that it is.

innovators. It provides a powerful countermeasure to the resistance and lukewarmness that innovating always encounters.

Innovating progresses iteratively, whether from concept to commercialization in the economic realm or from insight to transformation in the personal sphere. Multiple iterations of trials and errors—often called learning "loops"—progress through conceptual stages of development to the physical or "realized" incarnations of working prototypes. More often than not these learning loops are buffeted by the headwinds of rejection and resistance. "It'll never work." "It's too expensive." "We've already tried something like that before." "I am not smart enough." Autoimmune reflexes accompany and preoccupy the new wherever it emerges. New ideas are at first rejected. If there is no rejection, the idea is likely not new. Innovations are often considered impossible at first, based upon the conventional wisdom and accumulated knowledge as well as the entrenched interests of incumbents.

This pattern has been both observed and expressed in many different ways by many different innovators. One was Einstein, who put it this way: "If an idea does not at first appear absurd, it is probably not worth pursuing." But the assumption that God is One for whom all things are possible carries a profoundly hopeful implication into any innovating process. Whether innovators are conscious of their own tacit concurrence with this fourth assumption or not, the assumption seems to operate within them enough to work through the resistance and rejections they will surely encounter, both from within themselves and from their peers and sponsors. When this assumption is missing, it can have a debilitating effect on innovating.

When all four assumptions are taken together, innovators have something formidable with which to address the inevitable resistance and rejection that is so much a part of innovating.

There is another assumption that could be added to the four, though it is more anthropological than theological. This is the assumption that God gave humankind the freedom to choose, even to choose not to believe (in) God. It seems self-evident that were we not free to choose whether to believe (in) God and/or recognize the value of being in relationship with God, that we would be in a deterministic, robotic or mechanistic relationship with God. Being in a relationship where there is no such freedom or choice is really not much of a relationship at all. The relevance of this anthropological assumption to innovation shows up in the central role choice plays in innovating, perhaps as central a capability as creativity.

Other basic assumptions both theological and anthropological may eventually end up forming the foundations of innovation theology. At this embryonic stage, however, these four assumptions should provide the bare minimum.

INNOVATION THEOLOGY'S PURPOSE

Over the past thirty-five years of laboring with the innovating efforts of different companies in different continents, cultures and countries, I have observed *decreasing* interest in innovating especially on the part of incumbent organizations. Ironically *talk* of innovation has increased while investments in innovating have decreased. With all the talk, a shared and common understanding of what constitutes a genuine innovation itself has eroded. I am by no means the only one who has noticed the erosion. Many analysts suggest from an economic point of view that companies in the United States alone are investing in the future at the lowest level in some four decades, despite plentiful reservoirs of cash.[20]

One of the reasons may be a failure of nerve and an impatient desire for quick fixes.[21] I have seen firsthand leaders fail to even ask, much less answer, where and why innovations are needed from their own companies and in their own business ecosystems. Many leaders defer to others to both ask and answer these two most basic questions. Certainly there are exceptions. However, a significant number of innovation efforts, even ones attracting an abundance of financial capital, are neither structural nor infrastructural. Many are focused on quick fixes and quicker exits with big payoffs, from an app to a cleverly coded user interface.

The changes to which these "innovations" represent a response are not very substantive themselves. Rather they represent reactions to an uncertain future and reflect aims to skim off the surface rather than create new value rooted below it.

Short-termism chronically prevents leaders from asking where and why innovations should be pursued. Risk/reward ratios, net present value calculations or options-valuation schemes are all employed to calculate whether to innovate. These equations, however, are all far too weak to motivate authentic innovation efforts, even when these calculations do turn

20. Rubenfire, "CEO's Partly Sunny Economic Outlook"; Morath, "Secretary Lew Warns"; Christensen and van Bever, "Capitalist's Dilemma".

21. Friedman, *Failure of Nerve*, 2.

positive. The few highly publicized examples of entrepreneurial success with big financial rewards are often based on market capitalization more than profitability, much less the actual value contributed.

It is no secret most corporate ventures and entrepreneurial start-ups fail. Responding to change aimed at creating new value is difficult if not impossible to justify only on calculations and risk/reward ratios. The skepticism of investors whose motivations are more extractive and transactional than generative and relational is typically too great to overcome. Even those new entrepreneurial ideas that don't fail outright, even those that attract an acquirer's attention, or become "liquid" through an IPO, do so *before* demonstrating a profit or positive cash flow. Hindsight does not seem to influence much foresight. Financial markets have a way of distorting signals from economic markets, and even volatile extrinsic values have a way of distorting more stable intrinsic ones.

Entrepreneurs[22] with whom I have had the privilege of working typically *see and believe* in the value they can create and deliver to their customers well before they are able to calculate the returns with any confidence. These entrepreneurs are lining up the opportunities they see first with a point of view in plumb with a higher purpose, not a spreadsheet.

It is not that entrepreneurs shun financial calculations or ignore risk/reward ratios. Quite the opposite. They pay very close attention to the numbers. The bottom line is important. However, what calls them to risk failure and loss is that they *believe* in what they are doing and that it is worth believing in. This is a purpose greater than simply how much they stand to make at the end of the day. Greater purpose and other-oriented value is the central part of the equation in deciding to take the risk in the first place. This is fertile ground for theological exploration, ground wherein theology might plant seeds for answering where and why we should, could, can and need to innovate.

22. "Entrepreneur" has also morphed in its meaning. J. B. Say, the French economist, coined the phrase to originally denote one who took considerable risk to create resources and capital from sources and materials that were not generally recognized as carrying that value. Peter Drucker's discussion how "entrepreneur" is frequently misunderstood can be found in his *Innovation and Entrepreneurship*, 21.

PLUMB LINES VERSUS BOTTOM LINES

The prophet Amos had four visions. Of the four, the vision of the plumb line is perhaps the most memorable. Particularly remarkable is what Amos deselects in the description of what he sees. Here's the way Amos conveys it:

> This is what the Lord showed me:
>> the Lord was standing beside a wall built with a plumb line,
> with a plumb line in his hand.
> And the Lord said to me, "Amos, what do you see?"
> And I said, "A plumb line."[23]

If I was Amos and saw the Lord standing beside a wall, I would be hard pressed to focus on the plumb line. I would likely be more focused on the One who was holding it. However, when Amos replies with the simple "a plumb line," it is hard to miss the implication.[24]

Change can capture our attention but distract us away from what is most important. The intent of the plumb line is to hold up to us what is central and should not be missed. At the risk of overstatement, seeing the purpose of God may be even more important than seeing God. It is a simple yet potent image. The plumb line tightly weaves teleology (the study of purpose) and theology (the study of God) into in a single strand. With the aid of gravity, builders hold the line up to align whatever they are erecting to keep it straight and "on purpose."

The plumb line may have been envisioned first by Amos, but it certainly didn't remain captive of his prophecy. The intent of the plumb line runs throughout the entire prophetic tradition and even through the fulfillment of that tradition in Jesus. As a primary tool of measurement, the plumb line keeps our creative purposes aligned with and to the purposes of God. Plumb lines will likely be a "go to" tool of innovation theology.

Innovation theology cannot offer any magical potion to cure a failure of nerve. Nor are plumb lines substitutes for bottom lines. However, what innovation theology *can* do is encourage the entrepreneurially inclined to

---

23. Amos 7:7–8.

24. The prophetic plumb line concept will resurface in what follows. At this juncture, it is important to note that there are various pieces of core "code," or "instruction sets" that surface throughout the Old and New Testament (e.g., Jesus' self-understanding in Luke 4:18–21 wherein he quotes Isa 61:1–2 is one; Mic 6:8 is another.) Identifying what other plumb lines are particularly potent for innovators may itself be worthy of further development in any future innovation theology.

seek opportunity that is truly compelling. In fact, the purpose of innovation theology itself may be to challenge and enable the entrepreneurial leader to use a plumb line *before* using a bottom line to discern where innovations are needed and why. The stewardship, sustainability and social and economic benefit of our children's future depends upon it.

RESPONDING TO CHANGE NEEDS THEOLOGY

Globalization intensifies competition for raw materials. Commoditization erodes just about every competitive advantage. Democratization undermines every precarious political promise of incumbent administrations. Digitization disrupts stable institutions, with universities looking like the next institution on the cyber chopping block. Wave after wave of change pounds against the retaining walls of society, each wave weakening the political, economic and linguistic borders we were counting on. The effects of each storm are felt personally as well, in the particulars of disappointment, disillusionment, despair, loss, and alienation.

Despite the shelters we have built, private or public, in policy or psychotherapy, storms keep coming. Climates keep changing. The Irish poet, W. B. Yeats, prophetically described our situation this way:

> Turning and turning in the widening gyre
> The falcon cannot hear the falconer;
> Things fall a part; the centre cannot hold;
> Mere anarchy is loosed upon the world,
> The blood-dimmed tide is loosed and everywhere
> The ceremony of innocence is drowned;
> The best lack all conviction, while the worst
> Are full of passionate intensity.[25]

Volatility, turbulence, and uncertainty all seem to be increasing, perhaps even at an accelerating rate. Whether the rate really is accelerating may be debatable. But both sides of the debate would readily agree, we are living in an anxious time in an insecure world. The anxiety doesn't seem to be subsiding. Some of us are naturally prone to the more dramatic; others, more reserved. And surely our attitude toward change depends in part on how vulnerable we imagine ourselves to be. The mere threat of storms

---

25. Yeats, "Second Coming."

raises anxiety most everywhere, and the anxiety is not just about the storms but about what the future holds after the storms blow through.

Change is always in the forecast whether it's a weather, economic, market or personal forecast. And when change is in the forecast, stormy or not, we awaken to the fact that we will need to respond. Our responses can vary, to be sure. We can insulate ourselves *from* the change, accommodate ourselves *to* the change or we can innovate *with* the change. The degree of anxiety we have about the change will likely influence which response we choose. The more anxious we are, the less likely we will choose to innovate or respond generously to those who do.

I share Edwin Friedman's belief about the "rampant sabotaging of leaders who try to stand tall amid the raging anxiety-storms of our times."[26] Persistent "sabotage" shows up in countless forms of resistance to change and countless rejections of generative responses to it. Resistance and rejection are due not so much to the particulars as to the fact that the leader took initiative[27]—did something aimed at creating new value for others; in other words, when leaders attempt to innovate. This is one reason why we so often insulate or accommodate rather than innovate.

That theology speaks directly to "anxiety-storms" should not surprise us. Jesus not only stilled the waves and quieted the storm.[28] He was explicit in what he had to say regarding our anxieties in general and those tied to forecasts. "Don't worry about tomorrow."[29] Don't keep striving for what can be consumed. Don't keep worrying, for it is the nations (and companies?) of the world that strive after all these things, and your Father knows you need them. Instead, strive for his kingdom and these things will be given to you as well."[30] We typically understand these words personally. Seldom do we imagine that these words may be equally relevant to us organizationally.

What may be even more surprising, however, is that theology might also have something quite practical to say about innovating. While this may sound like a brash proposal it is based upon two assumptions: one about innovation and the other about theology.

26. Friedman, *Failure of Nerve*, 2.
27. Ibid., 3.
28. Mark 4:35–41.
29. Matt 6:25–34.
30. Luke 12:29–31.

INNOVATION

Those of us who have been laboring in the field of innovation for several decades have grown tired, even cynical, of the various uses and abuses of the word innovation, particularly of late. Once a word becomes widely adopted by the mainstream media its denotation becomes occluded by a great and vaporous cloud of connotations. Such is the perennial problem of language. But semantic mutation is particularly pernicious when it comes to words that become desolated by advertising messages. The words lose much of their precision.[31] Such has been the fate of the word "innovation."

As a result, at least for the sake of the following, innovation needs to be explicitly defined. A working definition that provides some distinctiveness in denotation while avoiding any obfuscating jargon is to define it as the *structural response to substantive change that aims to create new value*. Mindful that a response is not a reaction, what I intend to do with this definition is raise the bar on what qualifies as an innovation and an innovating effort.

First, innovating is a response to change. Clarifying this intends to avoid the frequent confusion of innovation with change itself. Internal change often becomes confused with external change; stimulus gets confused with response. When such confusion sets in, it is difficult to know whether you are communicating. Categorizing innovation as a response to change, at least for organizations, excludes something called organizational change (or change management) as a synonym for innovation. It is not. As important and necessary as organizational change can be, innovation is something else. Keeping the two separate avoids unnecessary confusion.

Second, by introducing the qualifier of "structural," I am intending to exclude much of what is constantly bubbling at the surface but remains superficial. To illustrate, consider the example of the iPod, often cited as an innovation. Taken by itself the iPod device was not really an innovation when it was introduced. It was another version of an MP3 player—something that had been around for a while. No doubt it was an elegantly designed device. But such elegance alone does not an innovation make. However, when the iPod is considered as one part of a system comprising an iPod, a service (iTunes) enabling music lovers easy access to music, and a new pricing structure that allowed not just albums but singles to be purchased, then the structural elements of the new system can be seen. This iPod/iTunes

---

31. McIntyre, *Caring for Words*, 12.

"ecosystem" *was* an innovation when it was introduced because it changed the then-current structure of music accessibility and delivery.

In the language of systems, when something new alters the structure of the existing system it is likely an innovation. When the degree of newness comes from adding or breaking structure it typically makes for a more seminal invention, no matter what the field. It may be worth noting here that invention and innovation are not synonymous. An invention-less innovation will likely not alter the broader system of which it is a part at a structural level, whereas an innovation with an invention more likely will.

Third, by using "substantive," the depth of change to which innovation is a response is qualified. The intent is to exclude changes that are superficial and transitory, along with responses to them that are also superficial and transitory. Many things that appear to be new are called innovations. However, many of these innovations are in name only. They are at best superficial. They reside only at the surface layer. Substantive innovations are typically more multilayered, structural or even infrastructural, causing restructuring at deeper layers of reality no matter what the domain.

Fourth is the "aim of creating new value" in this definition. Ever since Adam Smith's *Wealth of Nations*, economists have been fond of distinguishing between "exchange value" and "use value." Commercial innovations will find an exchange value, which, if sufficient, is often a measure of its financial success. When exchange value is insufficient, however, a potential innovation will be regarded as a commercial failure. Exchange value derives in part from the innovation's value in use determined by the perceptions and realities of the user or customer.

No matter how much use value the *innovator* may assign to the innovation, in the final analysis the *user* or customer has the final say, whether the innovator likes it or not. Suffice it to say that if there is a deeper intrinsic value associated with the extrinsic value then a greater purpose is present. In these instances we have a genuine innovation. Life-saving therapy innovations from the pharmaceutical and medical technology industries, or sustainable energy solutions may represent areas wherein the intrinsic roots of extrinsic value are easier to discern. In other areas, the difficulty of discerning the intrinsic values under the extrinsic ones shouldn't lead us to conclude that these deeper values are necessarily absent.

"Creating new value"—not merely adding, transferring or rearranging value—sharpens the difference between authentic innovation and its more trivial and superficial pretenders. This is not to equate creativity and innovation, though it does intend to imbue genuine innovation with some originality. What is regarded as original or creative, however, is inescapably derived from the subjective discernment of those who know enough about the domain to recognize something as new.[32] The community of knowledgeable practitioners is the only source qualified to appropriately apply the designation "new."

THEOLOGY

Delineating differences between theology and philosophy, cosmology, the sociology of religion, etc.—distinctions appropriate for a complete definition of theology—are beyond our scope. However, within the limits of my ability and this space, I would propose the following simple definition of theology—what some call reasoned discourse on God and divine realities. The definition is simply this: that *theology is what and how we explicitly think and express our experience of, relationship with and trust in, God.*

Part of my intent in defining theology[33] this way is to return theology to its rightful owners—you and me—not scholars, but laymen and laywomen, believers, and perhaps even a few agnostics as well. However we choose to classify ourselves and others, whether as atheist, agnostic or theist; whether Christian, Muslim, Jew, Buddhist, Hindu, or the more prevalent "I am spiritual but not religious," theology is in our thinking and speech, whether we are conscious of it or not. To "do" theology, therefore, is to examine explicitly what we implicitly experience of our individual and collective relationship with and trust in God.

Theology shouldn't be confused with religion. Religion is comprised of the shared beliefs, practices and traditions among a community of people who express and enact their orientation toward the Divine. Theology is, rather, the explicit expression of implicit belief. As explicit expressions of the implicit, the purpose of theology is to test the coherence, consistency, relevance and implications of these explicit expressions by means of reason and discourse. With whatever frequency we subject ourselves to these tests and whatever the test methodology, all of us express our implicit beliefs regardless of our relative confidence about those expressions.

---

32. Csikszentmihalyi, *Creativity*, 6.

33. The prominence and role of Scripture as a primary source for theology should be assumed, unless otherwise stated.

The point is that theology belongs to all of us and is practiced well or poorly by all of us. A hint of support for this premise resides in the repeated Gallup Polls that consistently tell us that over 90% believe in God.[34] This definition of theology is intended to be non-technical but specific enough to enable a reasoned consideration of theology's application into an area that could use it, namely innovation.

CONNECTION BETWEEN INNOVATION AND THEOLOGY

That innovation "needs" theology presumes some connection is possible between them. If innovation is left to the variable whims of its many media-hyped connotations and theology is mistakenly considered the exclusive province of scholars fine-tuning doctrinal propositions, then any connection between the two will likely elude us. However, if innovation denotes a deeper response to substantive change and theology stays close to its primary subject, the connectivity between the two begins to present itself.

There are several aspects to this connection. First, what connects innovation and theology has to do with choice. Choice is a thread woven into the fabric of innovation understood as response to change aimed at creating value. Choice is also central to theology as well. How choices are made, and even that we have the ability to choose, reflects a theological claim about free will. Choice deserves to be made more explicit before going any further.

When an individual or company *responds* to change it is reasonable to assume the respondent not only has a choice but also exercises it. Without the ability to choose (key to the ability to respond) change stimulates reactions more than responses. When one has a set of options and the ability to choose, but for some reason a choice is not made, the result is a reaction not a response. Only when one has a set of options, uses the capability to weigh the options, and selects from the set, can it be called a response.

What removes choice from an individual or organization is the absence of options, time or the capability to assess and weigh the options. For an individual, physical addiction is an example of lost choice. An active addict loses her ability to make choices, at least in regards to her will power

---

34. More than 90 percent of Americans believe that God exists. This figure has remained relatively constant since Gallup first asked the question in the 1940s. (Frank Newport, "More Than 9 in 10 Americans Continue to Believe in God," June 3, 2011, http://www.gallup.com/poll/147887/americans-continue-believe-god.aspx.)

to stop drinking or taking the addicting substance. As a result, the addict's ability to respond departs, leaving the addict to the mercy of her own reactions and reflexes. If and when abstinence is achieved the addict's ability to choose returns and the recovering addict can become response-able, at least more so than in the past.

Likewise for an organization, internal conditions or external circumstances can degrade the ability of leadership and management to make choices. This can happen when leaders perceive they don't have the time to generate and consider a set of options from which to select. David Packard called this a lack of digestive capability. The digestive challenge is wonderfully illustrated in an experience Packard recounts about the very early years of Hewlett-Packard. Packard confessed fondness for a truth he often repeated, but first learned from an unnamed retired engineer Wells Fargo sent to do due diligence on the young company. The occasion was the company's need for another round of funding. Because of the many opportunities the company saw in the rising tide of electronic measurement technologies, the engineer told Packard, "David, companies seldom die of starvation. More often they die of indigestion."[35] Indigestion is the risk of accommodation.

Such digestive inability could be a problem of fear, inadequate vision or a failure of nerve. All are likely suspects of this leadership deficiency. Whatever the reason, when otherwise responsible leaders give in to reflex or reaction they sacrifice both choice and the ability to exercise it. Having and making choices is central to responding to change. It is an essential ingredient of innovation, and essential to leadership.

Choice is an essential ingredient of theology as well. God gives us the freedom to choose whether we believe that God exists or not. If we so believe, we are free to choose whether we think God is actively engaged in the affairs of mankind or not. Just these two choices alone are filled with theological implications and consequences for how one chooses to live and how one chooses to view and relate to God. Theology spends much of its attention and energy in examining the implications, nuances and consequences of these choices.

Just as choice forms the logic of responding to change, the *theo*-logic of responding to change becomes more apparent when we realize that choice is shaped not only by circumstance and the available options, but also by purpose. When responding to change, sooner or later respondents must

35. Packard, *HP Way*, 57.

revisit their understanding of purpose. Without such a reexamination, the ability to make choices can atrophy or evaporate altogether. Theology and purpose are effectively inseparable, at least in the sense that theology is interested in God's purposes.

A second strand of the connective tissue between innovation and theology might be summarized in Viktor Frankl's often quoted observation that "between stimulus and response there is a space, and in that space is our power to choose our response, and in our response is our growth and freedom."

Innovators have a keen interest in this space and what happens there, as do theologians. The principles of innovation begin to be practiced in this space, as do the claims of theology. Theology will readily contend that God—the primary subject of theology—is not only present but also an active participant in this space. Prayer occurs in this space. Theology will also point to God's presence and participation outside this space, in both the stimulus that comes before and the response that comes after.

Those who believe God to be active and present in this space, and the spaces in front of and behind it, should readily see the theoretical and practical sense of the intersection of innovation and theology. Those who believe God to be a disinterested observer of this space will not likely see this connective tissue at all.

A third characteristic of this connectivity is in the underlying whys and wherefores of change. This is familiar territory for theology. New realities invisibly moving below the surface ("the deep") or emanating up from what is unseen are in theology's backyard, particularly when we consider the unseen and anonymous movement of God's Spirit. If it "sticks to its knitting," theology deals in matters that are unseen, under the surface, and anything but superficial. As a structural response to substantive change, innovation is also interested in what is below the surface at structural, infrastructural and ground layers of change.

A fourth aspect shows up in the practice of each. Centuries ago theology was often referred to as the "queen of the sciences"—a moniker that referred to its inherently interdisciplinary interest. Historically, separate fields of study comprise the content architecture of the modern university. This architecture evolved from Western European monastic institutions in the High Middle Ages (11th–12th centuries). As separate fields of study evolved, theology was often viewed as the integrator of them all. Theology has a long track record with deeper, broader "cross boundary" inquiries.

Just as theology is known for crossing the conceptual boundaries of different domains, experienced innovators recognize boundary crossing as native to innovating practice. Innovation simply refers to this in a more pedestrian manner as "connecting the dots."

In this respect, innovation and theology have similar proclivities for penetrating what is under the surface and widening the field of view to find dots to connect. However, just because there may be some intuitive connection between innovation and theology doesn't necessarily suggest innovation has an inherent practical *need* for theology. This claim deserves closer examination.

INNOVATION NEEDS THEOLOGY

To propose that innovation needs theology does not intend to imply a prepackaged solution theology has to offer to innovation. It intends, rather, to recognize that any response to change aimed at creating new value requires us to make choices within a context. Theology aims to understand God's purposes in a context. Where innovating needs theology is in the search to understand the *intrinsic* value within that context.

The domain of economics has held innovation in captivity for a long time. Economics is a field which many of its own practitioners admit may be much better at understanding the dynamics of supply and demand than the creation of new value. Unlike other economists, however, Joseph Schumpeter turned his attention to the creation of new value. Schumpeter, one of the more influential economists of the twentieth century, popularized the notion that near continuous innovation is more the norm than the exception. Schumpeter viewed capitalism as an evolutionary process wherein advances in society and economic well being happen as a result of a normative "creative destruction."

Thirty-five years after Schumpeter, Peter Drucker reexamined and revived interest in entrepreneurship and innovation. Though an economist also, Drucker's interests were more with the behavior of people than the behavior of goods, services and money.[36] A decade later, Clayton Christensen, also an economist, coined the phrase "disruptive innovation" reminiscent of Schumpeter's theory and reflecting the incumbent interests of his primary audience—leaders in established enterprises. These astute observers, along with many others, have made significant contributions to our

36. Drucker, *Ecological Vision*, 75–76.

understanding of entrepreneurship and innovation. However, even these thought leaders view entrepreneurship and innovation through the lens of economics.

To be fair, the field of economics provides much that has proven useful for managing innovating efforts. However, understanding innovation and entrepreneurship exclusively through the lens of economics is simply too limited. Drucker himself admitted as much.[37] Substantive change and our structural responses to it are too broad and deep to be confined to the domain of economics, corporate management or even one academic discipline alone. An economic lens on innovation may be necessary but is insufficient by itself.

Innovation practitioners themselves have for years looked to methods and theories from sociology, anthropology, relevant sciences and technologies in their quests to create new value. When it comes to understanding value—what really matters to people and why it matters to them—none of us can leave such understanding up to economists alone. Value, both intrinsic and extrinsic, is at the heart of the innovator's intent. This intent is called to the foreground when any of us respond to change, especially when the change is substantive and the response called for is more than superficial.

The notion of value in general can be sliced and diced in many different ways. However, when it comes down to what is important enough to hold our attention, capture our imagination and extract money from us, context plays the largest role.

Context—from the Latin *con* and *texere*, meaning "weave together"—is the surrounding set of conditions and circumstances. What shapes and determines what we value is the explicit or implicit purpose discernible in any context. The "text" of meaning is always tied to its context. Text and context are inexorably linked. When we lose, omit or forget an important piece of the context our view into the truth of the situation becomes partial or distorted. Have you ever had someone take what you said out of context?

Context, a seemingly innocuous word, turns out to be the silent partner in what makes value so much a part of the substance of innovation. The perennial challenge for any person or company responding to change, particularly an innovating response, is to turn an idea with potential value into a reality with actual value. In this effort, the starting idea will likely morph, even to the point of looking dissimilar to what it looked like in

37. Drucker, *Innovation and Entrepreneurship*, viii, 13–14.

its beginnings. The innovator must avoid ending up with an idea that is feasible but not valuable.

Theology too is keenly interested in this conversion of belief into relevant, purposeful and meaningful practice. Theology is interested in lives that are transformed from lives of less meaning to lives of more meaning. And when value or God are taken out of the context, theology reminds us, or should, that we are disabled. When value is "out of context," it has no value. It is only "in context" that it carries value. Selling refrigerators to Eskimos reminds us of the importance of context in shaping what is and what is not valuable. The intent of every innovating effort and innovator is to create new value. Here, specifically in the deeper notions of value theology is connected at the hip to innovation.

When God is taken out of contexts by implicitly assuming God is not involved or relevant, we have formed a conceptual boundary to the One who, whether we like it or not, is by definition not confinable to our conceptual boundaries. We take God out of the context, partly because God does not fit our concepts and frameworks. We take God out, leaving theology for the theologians, economics for the economists, and innovation for the innovators. This is all neat and tidy for conceptual categorization. However, its correspondence to reality is highly suspect.

Innovation's need for a theological perspective carries some urgency. The current bias of leaders to accommodate and insulate in response to change appears to be increasing. As I write this,[38] the *Wall Street Journal* posts a report of US Treasury Secretary Lew's remarks saying that companies are sitting on unprecedented piles of cash with a low or no investment mind-set. In this same month, the *Harvard Business Review* published an article by Clayton Christiansen decrying the outdated metrics driving CFOs to behave like cautious controllers, keeping the spigots closed on innovation investments. In the very same issue of *Harvard Business Review* former IBM CEO Sam Palmisano says the problem is not metrics but the maturity of management. Edwin Friedman, was less delicate than Palmisano.[39] He called it a failure of nerve more than a lack of maturity.

When it comes to choosing to innovate instead of accommodate or insulate, leaders lack sufficient theological imagination to understand the vocation (i.e., the divine and societal purpose beyond profits and shareholder value) of the organizations of which they are stewards. They may

38. June 11, 2014.
39. Friedman, *Failure of Nerve.*

also lack sufficient theological understanding in regards to the notion and responsibilities of a steward. In addition, the contexts leaders consider are often too narrow and parochial. Their choices too often ignore the under layers of intrinsic values from which extrinsic values derive. Consider all the technical and engineering talent, not to mention the massive amounts of private and public equity, being deployed on superficial innovations that are essentially digital platforms for more advertising. Shouldn't we be deploying these creative and financial resources to more substantive, structural and infrastructural solutions that address near crisis issues in energy, environmental healing and injustices displacing millions of people each year, injustices that exacerbate inaccessibility to basic food, water and shelter, not to mention medical care? There is some urgency to innovation's need for theology.

3

Accepting Change

CHANGE COMES IN ALL manner of sizes, shapes, and speeds. It can be massive or diminutive, widespread or local. It shows up in subtle shifts of ambient conditions, or in the pointed detail of particulars. It comes with sharp elbows or soft shoulders, and can feel like an impenetrable wall or a boggy swamp. It can approach slowly with advanced notice, or suddenly without warning. Change comes from seemingly out of nowhere, or from just around the corner, from the bottom up or the top down, or from all sides at once. Sometimes its causes are complex and at other times, a single underlying root.

With such variety it is almost impossible to define change in the abstract. Even within a single context what is called "a change" may be as much a function of the observer's subjective state as it is an objective reality. What is new to one may be just part of an old pattern to another. Point of view, perceptual distortions and an endless range of variations make it difficult to define where change begins and continuity ends. It is not so surprising then that about the only universal truth that holds about change is that it keeps happening. The ancient philosopher Heraclitus[1] observed that "no one ever steps foot into the same river twice." The constant thing about change is that it keeps changing.

---

1. That Heraclitus was sometimes referred to as the "weeping" philosopher may be directly related to his awareness of the constancy of change, requiring of him, presumably, a constant state or process of grieving.

As elusive as change is to describe, *accepting* change may be even more elusive. Accepting change easily succumbs to the inherent seductions of planning. A light-hearted, aphoristic riddle seems an appropriate place to start for such a difficult subject. It goes like this:

> Question: How do you make God laugh?
> Answer: Tell him your plans.

God's laughter may be more the knowing chuckle of a loving father than the uproarious belly laugh of a sardonic cynic. But regardless of how we might choose to describe God's sense of humor, the riddle reveals more about the persistence of our belief in planning than it does about God.

Planning is one of the more common and pervasive ways in which we deal with change, as individuals or as organizations. Our trust in planning and the methods we devise to predict an unknowable future may be as persistent as change is constant.

Consider for a moment all the intelligence we gather, all the data we mine, and all the technologies we invent for tracking and predicting. We spend an inordinate amount of time and energy anticipating, planning and preparing for changes that we cannot fully or reliability predict. We do this personally, corporately, nationally and internationally. Yet, we still have some difficulty *accepting* the change that seems to stimulate all this planning.

THE PROBLEM WITH PLANNING

Planning relies on predictions, whether explicit and formal or implicit and informal. Predictions are at best imprecise, at worst incorrect. Yet we keep predicting and planning. We justify this on what looks like an entirely reasonable assumption: if we can't stop change then at least we can anticipate it.

Anticipating change is not accepting it, but anticipating change can seduce us into thinking we are accepting it. "Hope for the best and plan for the worst," we tell ourselves, and then act according to plan. Conventional planning with its reasonable predictions works for the most part, at least for the more routine continuities of our lives. However, when change is substantial and our aim is to do something new, conventional planning can prove counterproductive.

Planning often reflects more of a desire to forestall, resist or mitigate change than to accept it. This is not to say that planning and predicting is not useful or necessary. Quite the opposite. Plans and the projections upon which they are based represent the foundation of prudent management practice, whether in our individual or organizational lives. Planning as far ahead as is possible provides us with at least some time to prepare. And such lead-times are especially important for innovating.

Ice hockey star Wayne Gretzky famously suggested that we must "skate to where the puck is headed." This is sound wisdom when time is short and space limited. However, few of us live in well-defined rinks with referees skating alongside, reinforcing rules others may forget. Most of us are saddled with the burden of having to navigate through much longer periods in more open fields with no one there to remind us what the rules are, if there are any, much less when an infraction occurs.

The probability of unanticipated events only increases as our time period lengthens and the scope of our horizon broadens. These longer periods and more porous confines make predicting speculative. This, in turn, makes planning and the plans it produces tenuous at best. As a result, planning is better viewed as a common form of coping with change more than really accepting it.

Over the years I have designed and facilitated a multitude of collaborative planning conversations in different settings and contexts. In each I have noticed two different orientations—one is anticipatory and the other is immersive. The anticipatory relies on projecting the collective imagination into the future. The immersive relies on experience that comes from jumping right in and getting a feel for what is going on now.

Each has its own inherent advantages and disadvantages. Anticipatory approaches look before they leap. In doing so they afford the opportunity to prepare—both for the leap and for the landing. However, these anticipatory approaches often lead to looks that prevent any leap at all. Fear sets in.

Immersive approaches, on the other hand, tend to leap before they look and in so doing create firsthand experiences from which to make further judgments and selections along the way. The risk with this approach however is that the initial leap proves to be a step from which recovery is difficult, if not impossible.

Anticipatory approaches produce plans while immersive ones produce plunges. The former produces predictive information, the latter produces experience-based data. Some balance of the two, if possible, is often to be preferred.

The unexamined assumptions we make about time are another problem with planning. Our language and culture affords us only one word and concept for time. The Greeks had two: *chronos* and *kairos*. *Chronos* connotes metered, regular, or predictable time, like hours in a day, days in a week, weeks in a year or even seasons of the year. *Chrono*logy is the temporal foundation of predicting. *Kairos* on the other hand means an opportune time, time with meaning, or as some say, "God's time." These are times when circumstances line up and intersect to make the moment, episode or period something more than merely another minute, hour, day, week or season. *Kairos* is time with significance.

Most conventional planning assumes *chronos*. Most innovating looks for *kairos*. When organizations attempt to innovate in a predictable and chronological way they end up with thin and superficial innovations. Results of these efforts require extra marketing and promotion just to garner recognition. When we innovate in *kairos* we seek new meaning and new value in changed circumstances and conditions.

The problem with *kairos* of course is that it is only apparent in hindsight. It is not certain in advance to the innovator. Only time (*chronos*) will tell whether now is an opportune time (*kairos*) for responding to change in a way to create new value. Hence, the only alternative to planning when our aim is to create new value is to remain alert to the potential value and opportunity in change.

This is not only a challenge for innovating. It is an age-old problem. Even Jesus and his disciples encountered it and to which Jesus' counsel was essentially "be alert at all times," "keep awake," because "about that day and hour no one knows, not even the angels in heaven."[2] Part of accepting change is acknowledging that we cannot know for sure what comes next or when.

Conventional planning is of little use to us when change demands a response that requires something new. Something else is required of us. It is not the "make it happen" mind-set of those who approach change with a command and control orientation. Nor is it the "let it happen" attitude of those resigned to *laissez faire*. Rather, it is to do our best to plumb the depths of the change, and then plunge in where it is already happening.[3] And our willingness to accept the change—even without knowing fully

2. Matt 24:36–44; Luke 21:7–36.

3. The second assumption—God is still creating—can imply that God is not necessarily waiting for us to engage in creating (see essay on theological assumptions).

what comes next—is likely stronger in the company of God. Such willingness is a prerequisite to a plunge that aims to create new value for others.

Those who study emergent systems have already begun to make a serious case for plunging in. Their reasoning acknowledges the limitations of traditional planning and its appropriateness for but a limited number of contexts. In this vein David Snowden has offered a useful framework. He calls it the *cynefin* framework.[4] *Cynefin* is a Welsh word that roughly translates as "habitat." The framework classifies at least four different change contexts in which we will find ourselves. Snowden calls them *obvious, complicated, complex* and *chaotic.*

Conventional planning might work in the obvious and even complicated contexts where conditions are either known or knowable. In these contexts we can with some effort approach change with a series of steps— first sensing what is happening, then categorizing or analyzing it, and then responding based on this analysis. However, not all contexts are that stable.

Other contexts have conditions that are so complex or chaotic that the conditions remain emergent and unknowable. Sensing and analysis just won't work. Instead, we must *do* something however modest. The doing of something produces feedback from the environment. And this feedback we can use for the next, more informed try or experiment. Snowden and others call these "probes" rather than plans.

Such probing may not be all that new. Martin Luther, who launched the Protestant Reformation in the sixteenth century creating complex if not chaotic conditions to be sure, seemed to have this immersive approach in mind when he offered his now famous advice to "sin boldly" as God is even bolder still.[5] Luther believed he and we would be acting in the company of God.

HORSE AND CART

When change is upon us two questions vie for our attention. "What are we going to do?" is typically the most urgent one. It often overshadows the other one, which is "What do we think is going on?" Answering the

4. *Wikipedia*, s.v. "Cynefin."

5. Luther, *Saemmtliche Schriften*, Letter 99, paragraph 13. "God does not save those who are only imaginary sinners. Be a sinner, and let your sins be strong (sin boldly), but let your trust in Christ be stronger, and rejoice in Christ who is the victor over sin, death, and the world. We will commit sins while we are here, for this life is not a place where justice resides. We, however, says Peter (2 Peter 3:13) are looking forward to a new heaven and a new earth where justice will reign."

more urgent question first has the unintended effect of overwhelming any answer to the other question, even to the point where the other question is never asked. Many have learned the hard way, however, that it is better to understand and accept the change before responding to it, at least as much as time will allow. This holds especially when the response calls us to create new value. Clarify what is emerging *before* choosing where and how to respond.

My own introduction to this principle occurred over three decades ago. I had been called to an important meeting. I knew it was an important meeting because all the vice presidents of the operating functions of Kimberly-Clark Corporation's consumer division would be there—manufacturing, marketing, sales, logistics, etc. Steve Wiley, the vice president of strategic planning had designed the meeting and invited me to facilitate the discussions. It was a three-day off-site held at the Four Seasons Hotel in Los Colinas, Texas. I was definitely the youngest, most junior person at this meeting, wet behind the ears. If anything went wrong, I was a handy, expendable scapegoat.

It was the middle of the morning on the second day. One of the more senior of the vice presidents, Jim Bernd, got up during the conversation to get another cup of coffee. After pouring himself a cup, he slowly turned and started to amble back to his chair at the conference table. Before he got to his chair, however, he interrupted the conversation and said, "You know, we do this kind of thing every year or so. We argue with each other, debate all the issues and end up eating too much and drinking too much. Then we come to some sort of agreement with each other that we all feel good about. But when we leave, and go back to our respective responsibilities, we all end up doing whatever we were planning to do before the meeting. Why do we keep doing this?"

Needless to say the meeting came to an abrupt halt. I did what any facilitator would do. I called a break.

During the break, everyone scurried off to pay phones (remember those?), grateful to have some excuse to avoid the awkwardness of the moment. Bernd, Wiley and I stayed behind and huddled together to try and figure out what to do next. It was clear that continuing as planned was not an option. The emperor—the meeting's agenda—had no clothes.

I listened quietly as these two senior leaders hemmed and hawed, back and forth. I could tell that neither one of them had any idea what to do next. Neither did I, but no one expected me to. Then, one of them said, "We are just not being honest with each other. We are not saying what we really believe."

The word "believe" caught my ear. I interrupted the two and said, without realizing the full import of what I was saying at the time, "Then let's just invite these guys to say what they really believe." When I said that the two of them turned and looked at me quizzically. It was Wiley who asked, "We can do that?" And I said, not really knowing, "Sure. I'll just ask them." And that is what we did. And it worked. For some reason, unknown to me at the time, the meeting and conversation transformed itself in front of our eyes.

A brief moment of honesty had occurred, a modest moment of truth, if you will. Perhaps it was because the one who spoke so candidly was toward the end of his career and willing to take a risk to point out that the "emperor had no clothes." Or perhaps, unlike others, Bernd had been through more cycles of this kind of planning than had others in the room. He just couldn't bear repeating the same unproductive pattern one more time. Perhaps there was something or someone else at work in this moment. Whatever the reason, what followed was clearly a more authentic and honest conversation, without a pre-envisioned or predetermined outcome. It proved cathartic to the leaders in the room, and transformative to the meeting and its results.

Prior to that moment we had had the cart before the horse. We were just following a process. In that brief moment the unperceived and unspoken was perceived and spoken. All it took was someone to tell the truth. People stopped posing in front of each other and started listening to each other. Each became genuinely more interested in listening and understanding the other than in being heard and understood themselves. They actually began to hear each other.

The moment was a brief crucible. It broke the prescribed process of the meeting. Otherwise powerful political rivals in the room expressed what they really believed. They heard differences in what each believed would happen and why. When differences revealed themselves the tragic narrative that had remained stuck in entrenched positions started to loosen up. All the various maneuverings of self-interests, hidden and not-so-hidden agendas, began to subside. The horse got back in front of the cart, partly because of Bernd's honesty, and partly because we started to address a different, prior question first—"What do we think is changing, whether we like it or not?" Coming to some common point of view on this prior question enabled us to ask and answer the "urgent" question ("What are we going to do?") more thoughtfully, clearly and coherently than before. But we could only do that *after* we had asked and answered the prior question—what do we think is going on? Moments like this turn out to be essential not only for accepting change but for creating new value as well.

At least three things happen when change is truly accepted: someone tells the truth, an old narrative gives way to a new one, and a catharsis occurs. We cannot hope to accept change or create new value in response to it without these three things—telling the truth, seeing a comedic future where before there was only a tragic one, and giving in to the catharsis that can transform us in the process.

We need to look closely at each of these, and a theological perspective proves to be a potent help in understanding all three.

TELLING THE TRUTH

Someone stepped forward and told the truth in this moment with the Kimberly-Clark executives. It was not just a "truth as I see it" kind of truth. It was a truth that everyone there immediately recognized and could no longer deny.

When someone—it only takes one—tells the truth like this it comes as a statement of the obvious. "Obvious" literally means "in the way." It may not really *be* obvious before it is expressed. It becomes obvious only after it is told, not before. But when it is, it becomes a truth that sets us free,[6] a liberation of sorts, not just for an individual, but for everyone else who is involved.

Who ends up being the one to tell the truth may not matter as much as the truth that is told.

However, the teller stands under the truth also and is just as subject to the truth as anyone else. In this particular instance, it turned out to be the oldest, most senior member of the group. Perspective and wisdom often comes with age and experience. But what matters more than perspective and wisdom is the truth's telling by one who is also implicated in the truth told. As such, it is a confessional kind of truth telling. Contrition is experienced and expressed. "A broken and contrite heart, O God, Thou will not despise."[7]

When a truth like this is told or confessed, it exposes a gap, the gap is between what is real and what is planned. This is especially the case with

6. John 8:32.
7. Ps 51:17.

predictions. When truth is told and heard, it has a way of revealing the distinct possibility that our view of reality—our truth—may not be the whole truth. Such truth can remind each of us that "now we see as in a mirror, dimly . . . now I [only] know in part."[8] Remembering this is humbling. It is also liberating. It produces a freedom for choosing to respond rather than react to change. This is genuine acceptance of change—when we are left with a choice and a willingness and readiness to exercise that choice.

Moments of truth create their own awkwardness, however. We don't really know what to say. We feel both a desire to break the deafening silence *and* a reluctance to say anything for fear it will sound superficial or be taken the wrong way. Before the awkwardness fades, the silence permits the truth to linger a bit longer. It is a truth that cannot be fully or finally understood so much as experienced.[9] Just for as long as the fading lingers there is a chance to accept the change named in the truth told. When told we catch a glimpse of the new realities and implied value that can be created in response.

There is something about the telling of the truth, the describing of it, the calling it out, that silences everyone. This includes the more skeptical, cynical and "Pilate" within or among us. Pilate asked Jesus, "What is truth?" And the silence that replied was deafening.

If Pilate's question was not rhetorical the silence that followed produced discomfort for Pilate as well. In fact it was so uncomfortable that he went back to those anxious for the reassurance of a plan, custom or protocol. And despite Pilate's admission that he finds "no case against him," Pilate chose the most expedient thing to keep the peace. Like so many leaders caught between a rock and a hard place, Pilate ignores the truth that even he sees, and follows the plan.[10] Many would say Pilate was just doing his job.

The experience of truth is fragile and temporary. Other competing truths, half-truths and illusions creep in. Doubt, skepticism and cynicism numb our taste for the truth, leaving us with indifference, even contempt. The educated ask, "Where's the data?" The sophisticated ask, "So what?" Like Pilate, the urbane cynically ask, "What is truth?" revealing less about the truth and more about their own disdain for anything not immediately aligned with what is expedient and pragmatic. Self-interest and postulates of plausibility weigh too prominently to permit much interest in truth.

8. 1 Cor 13:12.

9. Buechner, *Telling the Truth*, 21.

10. John 18:33–40.

Such moments of truth are of keen interest to theology, however, not only due to their revelatory affects but also because of their transformative potential. These moments are often turning points. Something new happens.

Moments of truth are of interest to innovation and theology, for much the same reason—their revelatory effects and transformative potential. In these moments innovators get to see and experience firsthand what is "in the way"—the obvious new realities change is bringing. A call and a need to create new value are embedded in these moments. Without these moments we give in to the anxious urgency to answer the "what are we going to do?" question. And in the process, we end up blind and deaf to what is right in front of us, and it is our plans that blind and deafen us.

The new realities change brings can be difficult to accept when we are in the thick of things. Though obvious in hindsight, the opportunity to create new value can be just as difficult to see as well. How many of us have asked, "Why didn't I think of that before?" and still failed to realize our plans and predictions were blinding us from the new? It is often the former things, the things of old, that prevent us from perceiving the new things that spring forth.[11] These former things are part of what we project into the future, the predictions upon which our plans are based. Moments of truth break through these former things and enable us to sense and accept the new.

We often give more attention to our plans than to the predictions upon which those plans are based. Sometimes all we can see is the plan. However, when we look beyond the plan and into the plausibility of the predictions those plans build on, what we find is an underlying narrative. All too often, without consciously choosing it, that narrative defaults to a tragic and deterministic one. This is a story line with an inevitability that reinforces the plausibility of the story.

Predictions are simply parts of stories we make up about the future. Sometimes we are conscious and deliberate about making up these stories. Sometimes we do so without realizing it. But whether conscious or not, the story lines we create serve our need for plausibility. We need to believe that there is a credible path from here to there, for how we get from current conditions to what is predicted, particularly if the future predicted is different than the present we experience. This is the same regardless of whether what is predicted is good news or bad. The narratives we imagine "fill in" the gap between our current reality and the future reality we envision.

---

11. Isa 43:18–19a.

The lesson here is that while our narratives about the future may be fictions, we often unwittingly treat them like fact. When we make and follow a plan we put our trust in a story we have created about the future. Making that story explicit is essential. This is more about story *creation* than story telling, though in the telling we can try out whether we believe it or not.

Plans express intentions. Intentions reflect assumptions about the future—always a fiction we intend to turn into fact. Therefore, it is not only prudent to consider the type of narrative that goes with our predictions. It is essential.

FROM TRAGIC TO COMEDIC

Narratives of the future, like all stories, have beginnings, middles and ends. In fact, the shape of the arc formed by the beginning, middle and end can indicate what type of narrative it is—whether tragic or comedic.

Tragic, deterministic arcs tend to move up before resolving in a downward trajectory concluding in some form of demise or death. Those looking for a repeatable formula, and especially those who believe they have found one, are at risk of telling themselves deterministic and tragic narratives about the future.

Comedic, improvisational arcs tend to move first down and then up, before opening up to something unexpected. The story ends in lift—an updraft more than a downdraft. The ending is life giving, not life ending. The narrative resolution of a comedic arc may not be as neat and tidy as what occurs in a tragedy. But the energy and attitude tend to be more attractive and attracting.

Innovation favors the comedic and improvisational more than the tragic and deterministic, as can theology. The gospel is bad news before it is good news. The movement of its narrative arc is down and then up. It doesn't end in demise and death but in resurrection and life. That theology and innovation share the same bias for the comedic should prove to be a resonance that nurtures a continued relevance for what theology might have to contribute to innovating.

Famously Nicodemus asks in response to Jesus' claim that one must be born anew, "How can anyone be born after having grown old? Can one enter a second time into the mother's womb?"[12] Nicodemus asked the question

12. John 3:4.

each of us asks when we sense our relevance is slipping away, whether as individuals or organizations. On the road to Emmaus Cleopas didn't recognize the resurrected Jesus. Stuck in a tragic narrative, Cleopas asks him incredulously, "Are you the only stranger in Jerusalem who does not know the things that have taken place there in these days?" Where have you been? And ironically, it turns out Cleopas is the one who is clueless.[13] Don't remember the former things, Isaiah says, nor even consider the things of old. "I am about to do a new thing; now it springs forth, do you not perceive it?"[14]

Nicodemus and Cleopas ask questions that come out of a tragic, deterministic narrative. Their tragic questions are answered from a comedic reality, however. Isaiah's question, on the other hand, comes out of a comedic, improvisational and open narrative. Was it Voltaire who described God as a comedian playing to an audience that refuses to laugh? Tragedy begins with a rise and ends with a fall. Comedy begins with a fall and ends with a rise.

The good news, for both theology and for innovation is that the truth comes not from a tragic narrative but from a comedic one. When moments of truth happen the truth has a way of relocating us "narratively." It tells us where we are, both in space and in time. We are not merely in chronological time (*chronos*) but in a time with meaning (*kairos*). And our task is to discover, uncover or co-create that meaning. And the value of the meaning and its hope is derived from the narrative. It is not necessarily where we want to be, or where we think we should be. Rather, it locates us where we actually are, in accepting the change.

Contrast this with conventional planning which favors more closed, tragic and deterministic narratives. Perhaps it is simply tragedy's penchant for closure or resolution. Or perhaps it is our desire to shun fantasies that are simply unrealistic. Fairy tales are entertaining but unbelievable.

Ambiguity and uncertainty are ultimately resolved in tragic narratives, more so than they are in reality. In comedic narratives ambiguity and uncertainty are the stuff of which surprise and improvisation are made. To traditional planning, ambiguity and uncertainty look like viruses. To innovation they look like fertile ground.

This is not merely the preference of the pessimist's view that the glass is half empty or the optimist's view that the same glass is half full. It is not simply a matter of attitude, disposition and outlook. Rather, it has to do

13. Luke 24:18.
14. Isa 43:18–19.

with a deeper, albeit often unconscious, commitment to the shape of the arc underlying the "account of the hope that is within us."[15]

When desire for precision takes precedence in our predictions—more than reality will reasonably allow—the consequence is a choice for a tragic, deterministic and closed narrative in our future. The more precise we imagine our plan needs to be, the more exacting our forecasts, the shorter the time frame and narrower the field of view.

This may work in operational planning contexts or when as individuals we plan more routine matters in more stable, controllable environments. However, it leaves conditions barren and desolate for innovating.

Plans can also distort the predictions upon which those plans are based. When the expression of our plan's intention takes precedence over an honest acceptance of change's new realities, plans begin to shape predictions, rather than the predictions shaping the plans. We succumb to self-fulfilling prophecies. The cart gets in front of the horse. Our interests and desires influence the predictions we make.

This is one reason that incumbent organizations find it so difficult to innovate. They become wedded to their plans and the implicit narratives upon which those plans are based. Often these are closed, deterministic and tragic narratives of the future. It's depressing, psychologically and economically. This same dynamic can hold for us as individuals. The more invested we are in the rituals, routines and desires to perpetuate our current realty, the more likely we are to miss the new realities change brings. We unconsciously default to an assumed future with a tragic narrative.

This brings us to another essential dynamic that happens in these moments of truth, wherein the plan often gets in the way of the truth, a truth that is absolutely necessary to perceive if we are to create new value for others.

A moment of truth is impossible to plan. It's more of gift received than an outcome achieved. Something happens to, with and among the participants. This "something" is what makes the moment significant. *Kairos* emerges out of *chronos*. The moment comes "out of" regular time and is recognized as special—a moment with meaning, primarily because a catharsis occurs.

15. 1 Pet 3:15.

TRUSTING CATHARSIS

Catharsis is a purging, purifying, cleansing and liberating experience.[16] Aristotle was the first to draw our attention to what a catharsis can do. He spoke about catharsis as the effect theatrical tragedy has upon an audience. According to Aristotle, tragedy leads to a catharsis or purging of pity and fear (*Poetics*). While it is not entirely clear whether Aristotle implied that the benefits of catharsis come only to theatrical audiences, it is clear that Aristotle saw in catharsis a way for us to regain a balance of emotion and perspective in our minds and hearts.[17] Both ancient spiritual practice and modern psychology (including Freud and others) picked up on the relieving and healing effect of catharsis and incorporated it in various treatment strategies. While Aristotle may have at first described catharsis as the effects of tragedy, subsequent thinkers have extended it to comedic effects as well.[18]

Catharsis is an uncomfortable but healing experience. What was repressed is finally expressed. Once expressed some relief is received. Then the hard work of transformation begins. Catharsis often happens within the context of a crucible—a heated experience through which a corrupting element is purged and the carrier is cleansed, typically not without some difficulty.

Crucible and catharsis are often confused. A crucible is a container that can withstand very high temperatures. Crucibles are used to hold contents—metal, glass or pigments—intended for purification. Catharsis is the cleaning and transforming process the contents go through in the container. Whatever the form of the container—crucible, cross, loss—catharsis is what happens to the contents inside. The container or crucible is not changed. The contents are.

Crucibles and catharses come in many different shapes and forms. The intensities of the heat and resulting purgation range from dramatic and emotional relief to mild and cognitive insight. But whatever the shape, form and intensity, catharsis leaves one changed for the better, not so much by personal achievement as by persistent sacrifice—the giving up of emotional attachments or intellectual preconceptions that no longer serve and are likely in the way.

Cathartic moments punctuate our individual and collective narratives of growing up, a growing up that never really ends. In my case, I was fortunate

16. *Shorter Oxford Annotated Dictionary*, s.v. "catharsis."

17. Powell, "Catharsis in Psychology and Beyond."

18. Scheff, *Catharsis in Healing, Ritual and Drama.*

to have a mother who would anticipate my passage through these moments by giving me a little tough love, saying to me often, "It's character building." This is a simple phrase that continues to prove true even long after she died.

Whether dramatic or incremental, catharsis results in a more emotionally balanced state from which a clear perception and willingly acceptance of change is possible. From a theological view, catharsis can transform an otherwise tragic narrative into a comedic one. The effects of catharsis are purifying and freeing at the same time. It relieves, heals and resolves. In so doing catharsis produces a clean and clear access to what is real, pure and true.

In purging one of pity, as Aristotle observed, catharsis leaves a capacity for understanding instead. It can turn pity and fear into understanding and hope, two capabilities that are coincidentally essential for creating new value. Here again, the interests of theology and innovation may naturally converge.

Catharsis cultivates empathy. "Empathetic identification with the end-user" is both an expression and principle well known and widely practiced by innovators. Understanding the need in context is one of the first things an innovator must do in creating new value.

Believing that one can fully "identify" with the other, however, has always seemed a bit presumptuous to me. Walking a mile in the shoes of another may help me to understand the other's experience, including how they feel and what they see from their point of view. But assuming that I can completely identify as the other not only takes something away from them. It also risks overestimating my own capability and under estimating the ever-present corruption of my own biases and points of view. And "empathetic identification" from an empathizer who has not experienced catharsis is likely to produce pity more than understanding.

Empathy may be an acquired skill, but without catharsis the intention and contributions of the empathetic can prove ineffective. Empathy can be a "power tool in the hands of the weak to sabotage the strong."[19] It can absolve the other of responsibility for getting into and out of the circumstances in which they find themselves, not resolving anything. Edwin Friedman makes the point this way:

> Empathy may be a luxury afforded only to those who do not have to make tough decisions. For "tough decisions" are decisions the consequence of which will be painful to others (although not harmful to others—an important distinction). The focus on "need fulfillment" . . . leaves out the possibility that what another may

19. Friedman, *Failure of Nerve*, 24.

really "need" is *not* to have their needs fulfilled, in order to become more responsible.[20]

Many attempt to practice empathy and end up with more "over-stand-ing" than understanding. This is partly because empathy is easier to describe than it is to authentically practice, and partly because, as Aristotle seemed to know, pity and sympathy are often substituted for understanding. This is a classic example of the good being the enemy of the best. Without experiencing catharsis an innovator may practice empathy[21] but produce very little by way of creating new value. Engaging without becoming enmeshed, and caring without taking freedom and choice *from* the other, requires an understanding born from one's own cathartic experience.

Creating new value requires accepting and understanding change in more than merely a superficial way. It requires not only changing our points of view. It requires allowing and trusting a change within our selves as well. This is the theological notion of repentance (*metanoia*—changing our way of thinking and acting). Einstein pointed to the same truth when he recognized that "the significant problems we face cannot be solved at the same level of thinking we were at when we created them."

Accepting change is not simply a cognitive reframing of our perceptions. It changes us inside as well. We can remain detached and objective for only a little while. None of us is immune to the penetrating effects of change. We cannot resist, deny and delay change forever. Those of us who have tried are likely to have learned how unworkable these strategies turn out to be.

Accepting change is not simply the job of recognizing the new realities outside of us. It is also an inside job, a change of our values and orientation. We may be able to change our point of view without experiencing a change within, but we are more likely to understand the other more deeply only after we have ourselves changed.

Innovation theology might come to suggest that the comedic often comes out of the tragic, that resurrection is only possible to those who have experienced death—a purgation of their own self-interests—so that they might live to and for the interests of the Other and others. In fact, it could be that with a theological point of view, a catharsis might actually transform a tragic narrative into a comedic one. Innovations themselves may be what results from cathartic transformations of organizations and individuals.

20. Ibid., 137.

21. All sorts of ethnographic techniques are currently in use to discover unmet needs among corporate innovators attempting new product development.

THE PROBLEM OF SELF-INTEREST

One of the few agreements among those who study innovation is that entre-preneurs seem to do it better than intrapreneurs. Start-ups innovate better and faster than ventures initiated by established companies. The evidence is overwhelming. Yes, there are occasional successes for intrapreneurs. But for the most part, innovations tend to originate where there is no internal (sibling) rivalry for resources. An incumbent organization's own self-inter-est gets in the way of giving full attention and complete understanding to the interests of others, for example, prospective customers. But while most agree, there is little consensus as to the cause.

You might think that with all the resources, knowledge and R&D of large, established companies, these organizations would show a better track record of innovating. Some attribute this dismal track record to pride that builds up before the fall.[22] Others believe it's due to the dilemma incumbent organizations cannot escape—"stick to your knitting" on the one hand, or "do something new" on the other.[23] Most view the problem from an eco-nomic point of view. A few view the problem as a lack of leadership. But none take a theological perspective—a perspective that has a decidedly dif-ferent take on self-interest than does classical economics.[24]

This dilemma is not unfamiliar to theology. A theological perspective will assume self-interest as a significant part of the *problem*. Theology can draw upon a rich set of narratives related to self-interest and sibling rivalries, not only with theological perspectives but practical wisdom. For transcend-ing self-interest there is always Paul's explicit counsel, patterned after the ex-ample of Jesus: "Do nothing from selfish ambition or conceit, but in humility regard others as better than yourselves. Let each of you look not to your own interests, but to the interests of others."[25] And for dealing with sibling rivalry

---

22. Collins, *How the Mighty Fall*, 2.

23. Christensen, *Innovator's Dilemma*, xiii.

24. Smith, *Wealth of Nations*, 485. Adam Smith's notion that individual pursuit of one's own self-interest will still be "led by an invisible hand to promote an end which was no part of his [the individual's] intention," has served as a foundational belief in economics for some time.

25. Phil 2:3–4.

we have to look no further than the stories of Cain and Abel,[26] Joseph and his brothers[27] or the parable of the prodigal son and elder brother.[28]

These are all narratives of hope, more comedic than tragic, more surprising and improvisational than deterministic and predictable. When we continue to think of innovation only from an economic perspective the prospects are dismal. Economics, on its own admission, is the dismal science.[29] It tends toward a tragic, closed and deterministic narrative. Theology deals in intrinsic values; economics in extrinsic ones.

Innovation is most often conceived of in terms of investment and return. However, if innovation is the creation of new value, it must first be valuable to the one the innovation intends to serve. Value to the provider or innovator depends upon value to the end-user or customer. This first value, theologically speaking, is an expression of love of neighbor and perhaps even love of God. In this sense the interest of the other is first and foremost, an interest other than one's own self-interest. As a result, should we be thinking of innovation as essentially a *moral* activity before it is an economic, technological or creative one? By moral I mean here simply the ability to consider interests other than one's own.[30]

From a theological point of view innovation itself might be viewed in an entirely different light—one that is keenly concerned with the love of God and the love of neighbor. In fact, is innovation even possible without some degree of altruism, some degree of putting one's own interests aside and giving oneself over to the interests of another? At first glance this sounds like a stretch. However, when one considers the animating power and freedom of God to do a new thing—the Doer being by definition the One for whom all things are possible—innovators may not want to dismiss this too quickly.

Understanding value is essential to innovating. If value is understood as extrinsic or exchange value then innovation will remain confined to an economic phenomenon. But if value is understood as intrinsic, if whatever the value is and however it is embodied, is truly valuable to the one for whom it is intended, then is it not possible that innovations are

---

26. Gen 4.

27. Gen 38–47.

28. Luke 15:11–32.

29. Thomas Carlyle in the 1849 tract called *Occasional Discourse on the Negro Question* was apparently the first to refer to economics as the "dismal science."

30. Niebuhr, *Moral Man and Immoral Society*, xi.

embodiments of love of neighbor? Regardless of the commercial transactions associated with the buying and selling of this value (a transaction that can and does erode the love for which it was created) is it still not, at least in intent and design, an expression of love?

This may hold true for individuals but may not for organizations. Reinhold Niebuhr made a powerful case for this difference in his classic *Moral Man and Immoral Society*. Niebuhr observed that

> individuals are capable of preferring the advantages of others to their own . . . a rational faculty that prompts them to a sense of justice . . . but these achievements are more difficult, if not impossible, for human societies and social groups. . . . In every human group there is less reason to guide and to check impulse, less capacity for self-transcendence, less ability to comprehend the needs of others and therefore more unrestrained egoism than the individuals, who compose the group, reveal in their personal relationships.[31]

Niebuhr's skepticism regarding the capability of any organization to behave morally strikes many as unduly cynical and pessimistic. But if Niebuhr is even partially correct, it may go a long way to explain the mystery of why existing organizations have more difficulty creating new value than do new ones.

Even if we disagree with Niebuhr's skepticism, theology clearly has an interest in the love of God and the love of neighbor—two distinct but inseparable realities according to most theologies rooted in the biblical saga. Cain's question ("Am I my brother's keeper?"), the parable of the Good Samaritan, Jesus' summation of the whole law, and much of the biblical library is concerned with these two realities—two realities that arguably form a foundation for any theology.

So, what of self-interest? Jesus' citation of the second great commandment—"love your neighbor as yourself"[32]—assumes that we love ourselves before we can love our neighbor. When this assumption does not hold, as under conditions of shame, it becomes practically difficult to love our neighbor or anyone else for that matter. Love, here, of course, is not limited to just a feeling. It is a creative act which when done selflessly, creates value for the other.

French philosopher Auguste Comte was the first to coin the term "altruism." It represents the opposite of egoism or self-centeredness. The

---

31. Ibid., xi, xii.

32. Luke 10:27; Matt 22:39; Mark 12:31.

human motives underlying altruism are still being debated, at least within the frames of psychology. One side holds firm to the position that humans have an inherent, selfless capability, while the other side counters that what appears to be a selfless act really benefits the giver and is therefore motivated out of self-interest. Whether neuroscience will bring any resolution to the debate may not be known for some time. However, theology has likely never found much to debate. The close coupling of the love of God and love of neighbor leaves little room for isolated or individualistic self-interest.

Direct experience confirms this. When we give without thought of a return and even anonymously, it feels good. The good feeling may be one of relief, a reprieve of sorts, with an otherwise lingering preoccupation with ourselves. Or the good feeling may be due to an inherent alignment with the love of God and of neighbor. At the very least, when we are fully engrossed in doing something for someone else, without expectation of any return, we are relieved of the distractions from any self-interest. Creating new value for another seems to require this. Self interest makes it difficult for established organizations—concerned with protecting and defending what they have going—to take the risks to create something new and valuable for others.

However we view altruism, whether a form of self-interest in a clever disguise or the God-given capability of individuals, theology certainly makes it clear that this love of neighbor is inseparable from the love of God and a central reality of anyone in the company of God. The question is what we do with whatever lingering self-interest is there. This is not simply a problem that confronts the religious. It confronts organizations trying to innovate and individuals trying to accept change. But here, theology has something to offer as well. It is the radical message of *kenosis*.

THE "SOLUTION" OF KENOSIS

Kenosis is a Greek word that denotes "emptying" and a theological principle that takes a radical position regarding self-interest. *Kenosis* is used in one of the earliest creedal affirmations of the early church. Found in Paul's Letter to the Philippians its beauty and potency is as striking as its truth is timeless and profound:

> Do nothing from selfish ambition or conceit,
> but in humility regard others as better than yourselves.

Let each of you look not to your own interests,

but to the interests of others.

Let the same mind be in you that was in Christ Jesus,

who, though he was in the form of God,

did not regard equality with God

as something to be exploited,

but emptied (*kenosis*) himself,

taking the form of a slave,

being born in human likeness.

And being found in human form,

he humbled himself

and became obedient to the point of death—

even death on a cross.[33]

This truth has survived generations of experience shaped by many crucibles animating many cathartic moments. It continues to do so. Going into those crucibles are tragic, deterministic narratives. Coming out of them are hopeful, open, improvisational and even comedic ones. Forget the former things, the old ideas. God is about to do something new. Even now it springs forth. Don't you see it?

The value of every innovation resides in the interest of the other—the one for whom the innovation is intended. What the other finds valuable, what is useful to them becomes explicit at the moment of birth for any commercial enterprise. It is the moment when it attracts and retains its first paying customer. The payment is a sign and seal confirming value has been recognized if not realized.

The extrinsic or exchange value—the price the company charges the customer—is derivative of value the customer assigns to the product or service. Whatever ends up being the price-value relationship, however, it was an interest in the other that started the whole ball rolling in the first place. This interest in the other is intrinsic before it takes on an extrinsic quantification. The interest of the other is not only the heart of innovation. It is the heart of a business as well and the company that provides it. Love of neighbor.

Self-sacrifice, including the sacrifice of self-interests, is essential if something new and valuable is created for another. And when such new

33. Phil 2:3–8.

value is created, it transforms what is otherwise a tragic, deterministic narrative into a comedic, improvisational one.

It is easy to lose sight of this basic interest in the other, especially when businesses grow. Success, ironically, born out of a basic interest in creating value for another, without which there would be no business to begin with, ends up creating a lot of self-interest as well. And as self-interest grows it can often overshadow the interest in the other. Walt Kelley (d. 1973) must have had something of this in mind in his creation of the comic strip character *Pogo*. One of the more famous of Kelly's cartoons had Pogo speaking from the Okefenokee Swamp: "We have met the enemy and he is us."

Planning itself can get in the way of creating new value for the other because this innovating requires the ability to put aside one's own self-interests in order to focus on the interests of others. Plans have a way of carrying forward the self-interests of either the one doing the planning or the organization for which the planning is being done. In the context of a commercial enterprise, the organization can grow to such a size and complexity that the interests of the organization become more important than the interest of the customers—the ones the organization intends to serve.

As organizations grow and age, many suffer under the weight of their own size and complexity. An increasing amount of effort is spent maintaining what the organization has going rather than starting something new. Self-interests, from the organization's point of view, become as important as the interests of the customers they serve. As individuals grow older, many suffer under the weight of their own experience, loading their memories and shaping their expectations, neither of which are as loaded or shaped in the young.

This is where the role of imagination enters into the challenge and process of accepting change, especially empathic imagination.

4

Reimagining Change
From Wound to Invitation

THE ROLE IMAGINATION PLAYS in innovating is as widely recognized as it is poorly understood. How we imagine change and our response to it is one of the few things than we can effect, an effect to which theology makes a significant contribution. The role and contribution imagination plays is significant and worth looking at more closely.

All the discovering, inventing and solving that goes on in innovating efforts requires imagination. Imagination is also essential for accepting change. However, not all imaginations are equal or work the same. Neither are imaginations merely intellectual. Imaginations are endowed with emotion, can be wounded by the losses that change inflicts, and yet, can grieve and heal. Much innovating fails, however, even with the application of creative individual and collective imaginations. Even brilliant and knowledgeable imaginations can be wounded. But responding to change with healed imaginations can lead to better innovations. Grieving the loss of what was frees us to respond to what is. When we are thus freed, we are enabled to create new value; in other words, we are free to innovate.

The late Edwin Friedman tells of a nurse who came across a biological fact in a medical journal that caught her attention. It reads this way:

> When a wound occurs there are two kinds of tissue that must heal, the *connective* tissue below the surface, and the *protective* tissue of the skin. If the protective tissue heals too quickly, healing of

the connective tissue will not be sound, causing other problems to surface later, or worse, never to surface at all.[1]

When change is significant, it cuts through both the protective and connective tissue of our lives. Penetrating changes of this sort require structural and substantive responses which themselves heal both protective and connective tissue. Superficial responses run the risk of denying, delaying and distorting responses required for healing at a deeper, more sustainable level.

Responses to what is below the surface may arguably deserve more of our attention than those on the surface, but we should be cautious here. Healing is necessary in both protective and connective tissue layers. This is what caught the eye of Friedman's nurse. One layer affects another. What appears superficial can have surprising effects on the more substantive.

Anxiety might focus and motivate the mind on change and its implications, but anxious concern also amplifies dis-ease. From hundreds of collaborative problem-solving efforts in various industry and organizational settings I have repeatedly observed anxious imaginations grappling with problems before the anxiety subsides. This is far from optimal. Anxiety can distort and even cripple imagination. It tempts imaginations to get to a solution quickly—a fix more than a solution, really. For example, when organizations and individuals realize they don't have something in mind, or what is "in mind" is not possible, a rush ensues to whatever anxious and defensive imaginations may conceive. What gets conceived is often mislabeled "innovation," partly as a way of justifying it. Giving in to this temptation leads to quick fixes.

We are chronically impatient problem solvers, quick to get to a solution. Many false starts, abandoned efforts, and lots and lots of failure litter innovating landscapes. In our rush to solve we leave losses un-grieved. This pattern of behavior may be the root cause of the difficulties individuals and organizations have in their respective attempts to respond to change.

Substantive change is happening on many horizons. Environmental examples might include the threatening effects of climate change or the looming shortage of water. For economic landscapes it may be the disturbing growth of inequities of income. On personal landscapes it could be divorce, death of a parent or even worse, loss of a child. There are countless other examples here as well. Losses like these penetrate through protective tissue and slice into what holds things together underneath.

---

1. Friedman, *Generation to Generation*, 45.

Mental images of change form early, even subconsciously. What we imagine and how we imagine it is shaped by our unconscious prevailing mind-set.[2] It is like the proverbial fish out of water. When out, it becomes aware of the water it was in. Similarly for us, it is difficult for us to be aware of our own mind-sets, unless and until we are taken out of them, as when we visit another culture and catch a glimpse of what is peculiar about our own.

Our imaginations reflexively form images of change quickly, too quickly. Reasons for the quickness can be explained from a psychological, neurological and theological perspective. A psychological perspective might compare and contrast fixed mind-sets with growth mind-sets.[3] A neurological perspective on imagination might suggest that imagination does not happen only in the brain, but in a more distributed fashion.[4]

A theological perspective will take a different view. One such perspective comes from what Old Testament scholar Walter Brueggemann calls the "dominant" and "prophetic" imaginations.[5] Brueggemann finds these two types of imaginations saturating the Hebrew Scriptures, influencing the New Testament Scriptures as well. Thanks to his brilliant exegesis, Brueggemann's prophetic and dominant imaginations serve as the primary architecture for this essay, the point of which is that four different types of imagination are required of us when responding to change: *dominant, prophetic, emancipated* and *innovating* imaginations.[6] When we *react* to change we are employing only one of these imaginations—the dominant. When we *respond* to change, however, we employ all of them.

A brief definition of each imagination is necessary here.

- The *dominant imagination* views change defensively as a threat more than an opportunity. Self-interest[7] is at the heart of the dominant imagination. This imagination tends towards conservation and preservation more than innovation.

---

2. Meadows, *Thinking in Systems*, 162–65.

3. Dweck, *Mindset*, 2–14.

4. Wilson, *Hand*, 39.

5. Brueggemann, *Prophetic Imagination*, xix.

6. These four represent an expansion on Brueggemann's two—prophetic and dominant—though even Brueggemann seems to allow for the third—the emancipated imagination. Should my improvisations corrupt Brueggemann's forceful and persuasive biblical scholarship, the mistakes are mine, not his.

7. Whether "self" is an individual or an organization.

- The *prophetic imagination* critiques the dominant imagination and views change as evidence supporting its criticisms. Deeper purpose and intrinsic value (e.g., love, justice) is at the heart of the prophetic imagination. This imagination is focused on what is real and true in what is changing.

- With the window opened by the prophetic imagination, the *emancipated imagination* is freed to envision what might be possible. Interest in others and in closing the gap between what is and what should be (i.e., justice, righteousness) is at the heart of the emancipated imagination.

- A liberated imagination can lead to the *innovating imagination*. The innovating imagination is interested in what is possible now. At the heart of the innovating imagination is what can be embodied or realized in the present—new value that narrows the gap between what is and what should be.

Innovating imaginations are unlikely to get beyond the superficial without the prior work of the prophetic and emancipated imaginations. Imagining what is possible now without the prophetic breaking through the dominant and without expanding the field of what is possible, leaves us too often with superficial innovations.

The current tools of neuroscience, including brain-imagining technology, are woefully insufficient to give us evidence with which to measure or describe how the imagination actually works, much less why.[8] However, neuroscience has confirmed that thinking and feeling are inseparable. Imagination always works with and through the amygdala where emotions are processed. This is but a reminder that a healed imagination is not simply a function of neuronal circuitry, but is also a matter of emotional balance and spiritual purposefulness. A whole and healed imagination is more than just what's in your head or how you "process information." Healed imaginations, theology might suggest, are those free to imagine what the One for whom all things are possible might be capable of choosing in the creation of new value.[9]

---

8. Conversations with marine biologist and neuroscientist, Dr. Stuart Thompson (Stanford University), and Dr. Stuart Brown, MD (National Institute for Play—play science).

9. Taylor, *My Stroke of Insight* (TED Talk).

A constant temptation for the innovator is to sacrifice what is possible on the altar of what is probable. Invention becomes a burnt offering on the altar of convention, or what is most excelling on the altar of what is more expedient. The dominant imagination will reasserted itself when such sacrifice is made. When this happens we forget or degrade much of what the prophetic and the emancipated imaginations have brought. The temptation is strong. Why not dispense with all this talk of grieving loss and embracing the critique of the prophetic? Who really needs to widen the field of view and consider what might be possible with an emancipated imagination? What we really need is a feasible solution. Let's get practical and go right to it. The need is urgent. Who can argue with this logic?

This is the point where it may matter the most whether we are in the company of God or not. Healing does not happen without engagement of both connective and protective tissue. Regeneration repairs what was torn in both protective and connective tissues. Restoration seeks completion. But once restored we can easily ask, for what purpose now?

LOSS AS POTENTIAL ADVANTAGE

Change affects the deserving and the undeserved. Losses always accompany change, whether anticipated or incurred. I have learned this firsthand as a lab rat in the many and varied experiments of my own life. Even welcome change brings necessary losses.

Our attitudes toward loss are difficult to separate from our orientation to change. Research in decision-making strongly suggests that most of us would rather avoid loss than risk gains.[10] This preference for loss avoidance makes it more difficult for us to accept change, and so we prefer conservation or preservation rather than innovation.

A conservation mind-set estimates what remains in the reservoir, compares this with the current rate of drain, and forecasts when the reservoir—money, time, knowledge, etc.—will be used up. The basis of the comparison is a projected gap (anticipated loss), and its purpose is to save resources, or prolong the life expectancy of the reservoir. A conservation mind-set pays attention to the volume of the resource supply and the rate at which it is being used.

---

10. Daniel Kahneman and Amos Tversky developed prospect theory—a seminal theory in behavioral economics—for which they were award the Nobel Prize in 2002.

A preservation mind-set looks at loss differently. Preservationists are more interested in the purity, quality and character of the content than the level of its volume. The preservationist seeks to protect the purity of what's in the reservoir even more than save its quantity. The preservationist sees the content as worth preserving in its original state. Loss for the preservation mind-set is a loss of essence or purity or character—loss through contamination or corruption.

An innovation mind-set looks at loss still differently. For this mind-set, losses are a symptom of change more than a gap in supply or a corruption of purity. While still losses, the innovation mind-set sees in the loss a telltale to what may be a better, as yet unseen and still uncertain future. As this mind-set has a purpose of creating new value, losses will necessarily be viewed in this light.

Some might think of this view of loss as Machiavellian, lacking in compassion. And to some degree this criticism is warranted. However, it does have the advantage of viewing losses of any kind not as something to prevent, delay or guard against. Loss actually becomes a part of the new set of conditions, even a potential asset.

This is a completely different orientation to loss. Conservation and preservation view losses as essentially negative, things to resist, slow down, and protect against entirely. An innovation mind-set tends to view losses as an inevitable part of change. This attitude toward loss demands emotional intelligence,[11] one that views loss as not only inevitable and constant, but a signal to pay attention to, if not an invitation to accept.

This is not to imply innovation should be preferred over conservation or preservation. All three represent viable responses. Rather, it is simply to acknowledge that loss is an inescapable consequence of change, and as a result, our attitudes and strategies for dealing with loss are worth examining. Once grieved, loss can become an advantage, and change, an invitation, to create new value for others.

---

11. Bill Wilson started Kimberly-Clark's early disposable diaper business on a research budget. Wilson demonstrated high emotional intelligence when Jack Kimberly told him directly to stop work on diapers because of all the losses. Bill kept working—with his team—on diapers. Bill's persistence proved to be arguably the most productive act of insubordination in Kimberly-Clark's history. Diapers remain the company's number one profit maker. Cheverton, *Maverick Way*.

CHANGE AS INVITATION

Many view change as an interruption, a loss of continuity, if you will. As a variation from the norm change brings with it something different. It interrupts the flow of things, never mind that the flow itself might be seen as change. It's perceived as a divergence from what has been and what was expected.

Of course, the same can be said about innovation. It brings something different, is a variation from the norm, and diverges from what was expected. Both change and innovation can *appear* to be interruptions, even "disruptions." As such, both change and innovation often can and do take negative connotations.

However, change can be viewed in a more positive light. When present circumstances may be less than desirable change can bring welcome relief. And even if change brings no obvious relief, it can be seen as an invitation, if we so choose.

If we assume that God is still at work, still creating, then the changes we experience could just as well reflect this ongoing work as not. It could represent a divine invitation. Innovation theology may end up biased toward the possibility that change represents an invitation.

Consider this hypothesis: *change may deliver a divine invitation to freely, fully and creatively participate with the company of God in creating new value for others.*

First, by *change* I simply mean significant external movement and differences emerging in the natural, physical, societal and cultural environments in which we live, as individuals and as organizations. I am not so much referring to internal or psychic change as I am external changes to which sooner or later we will be required to respond (or react).

Second, by *divine invitation* I mean to imply vocation.[12] A more conventional expression might say that God "calls" us to respond. Saying that in change God *invites* us to respond fits a bit more snugly with the character of change. The relevant word in Scripture (*kaleto* in Greek) is and can be translated either as "call" or "invite," depending on the scriptural context in which the word is used and the translators' judgments.

Freely has to do with God's desire for us to choose whether we accept the invitation or not. The choice is ours. This has a direct bearing on

---

12. Vocation, from the Latin root *vocare*, means voice. It is often translated "call" or "calling." Both imply a someone rather than a something—one who has a voice, one who calls to others, a caller. Unfortunately, vocation is often fused with career only.

innovating effectiveness. A voluntary attitude turns out to be essential to innovating. This is one reason employees have difficulty innovating. Likewise, *fully* has to do with whether we are lukewarm or all in. This is another characteristic typically regarded as essential to innovating and of likely interest to God.

Co-creative participation intends to imply what you might think—a collaborative activity between God and people. In other words, we get to participate in God's creating if we so choose by accepting the invitation.

And finally, *the company of God*—an expression I intend as a vernacular surrogate for the kingdom of God on earth and in our world—reflects the collaborative community of others, all of whom are stakeholders in the purposes of this company, regardless of the degree of their awareness of the company's presence and purpose.

As an interruption change is negative, an inconvenience at best, an invasion at worst. Responses to interruptions tend to be begrudging—something we *have* to do, not something we *get* to do. They take the form of reluctant compliance. "We have no other real choice." Though we may be able to delay our response, sooner or later we know we will have to attend to it. Such a response garners the least amount of effort. We really would rather get back to whatever it was we were doing.

As an invitation however, change can *call* us to reconsider the trajectory of our present course. Surely when we are invested in keeping things the way they are we can miss the invitation entirely. But when we can no longer ignore or deny the change, reassessing where we are and where we are headed becomes the only appropriate, rational and prudent thing to do. In this view, change itself can extend an invitation to us to rethink and reconsider.

Bring a theological perspective to change, and it will naturally cause us to ask where, or more accurately, from whom the change is coming. Inconvenient or irritating interruptions may just possibly be divine interruptions. Receiving an invitation from a living, still creating, loving One, for whom all things are possible, may cause us to respond differently.

If a *loving* God is the source of change, then seeing God as a host inviting us as his invited guests makes sense. This perspective can transform change as wound and loss into change as invitation and opportunity. Put another way, if God is the host who sends out invitations embodied in the changes we encounter, then we may be on God's guest list. And if we are on his guest list, then this implies the host would like us there, participating, contributing, co-creating with God in this ongoing work.

The default mode for many is to view change primarily as interruption. In this mode, our readiness to innovate will lag. Reasons for this come from our investments in extending and defending the *status quo*—as individuals and organizations. Investments in our self-images may be another reason. These self-images reflect who we think we are in the context of our more familiar current realities—identities drawn from our work, our roles in families, organizations, churches, etc.

But when we turn from change-as-interruption to change-as-invitation, our response can easily move from one of begrudging obligation ("I *have* to do this") to voluntary willingness ("I *get* to do this"). Perhaps even more importantly, our attitude shifts from receiving the new realities of change as bad news to receiving these new realities as good news, particularly when we consider from whom the invitation is coming. In short, when we view change as invitation, we are more likely to at least take a closer look at the opportunity to create new value for others.

GOD INVITING

When change and our response to it is viewed through a theological lens—as a divine invitation rather than an inconvenient interruption—we begin to understand change and our response in a new light. We can see our response more clearly as a commitment to show up, freely, willingly and fully to participate in what the Host has prepared for us. If God is still creating then what the Host is preparing for us in change is chance to contribute. Viewed as an invitation, change carries at least the possibility, if not the probability, that the Host not only wants *us* to show up, but will be there as well.

The freedom of the invited to accept or decline is implicit. An invitation is not a requirement or a command. It is an invitation. Accepting or declining the invitation has its own consequences and costs, to be sure. However, when a genuine invitation is accepted it is reasonable for a host to assume that the invited show up *wanting* to be there. The invited willingly participate without obligation or coercion. The desires of a host and the desires of the ones who accept come together. This is a potent union, particularly for creating new value.

Most veteran innovators recognize that a free and voluntary mind-set is essential for innovating. In contrast, an employee mind-set often proves insufficient. Without voluntary acceptance of change, many end up viewing themselves as victims of change, compelled or coerced by circumstances. Willing acceptance, however, enables us to be fully present for responding.

When the response aims to create new value, nothing less than our full attention and presence will do. When strings are attached, obligation easily creeps in. Compliance comes to shape the presence and posture of the invited. Participants compelled, coerced or under some external compulsion to show up, end up less prepared, less present, less giving and less committed to the occasion and to the host. For those who are not there under their own volition, the occasion is an inconvenience, an intrusion and ultimately, an interruption.

Sometimes acceptance implies that the invited will prepare.[13] At other times the only preparation possible is to show up. But whether prepared or not, an invitation implies that a host has prepared something ahead of time. This is not far from the common belief that God has plans for us, and with such a plan come practical implications.

JESUS' ATTENTION TO INVITATIONAL DETAIL

The practical implications of invitations are nowhere more apparent in Scripture than in the fourteenth chapter of Luke. Here Luke weaves together three distinct vignettes with Jesus saying something about invitational behavior in each. The detail with which Jesus looks at invitations is striking. Perhaps one reason for the intensity and granularity of Jesus' interest in these invitational dynamics here is because these vignettes precede his enumeration of the onerous costs of discipleship. The consequences of accepting and following through on the invitation can be significant if not severe.[14]

Responding to change with an aim to create new value is not for the faint of heart. The consequences of acceptance are significant and demanding. For those who take up the challenges of discipleship or for those who take up the challenges of innovating, the sacrifices required and the consequences experienced are dear. Many are invited. Few follow through. In the company of God, however, God can and will do for us what we cannot do for ourselves.

---

13. Matthew's version of Jesus' parable (Matt 22:11–14) reveals what might happen if one accepts the invitation and is not prepared, or at least appropriately dressed for the occasion.

14. Luke 14:25–33, where accepting and following through on the invitation to follow Jesus means (1) hating those closest to you and even your own life, (2) carrying the cross, and (3) giving up all of your possessions.

Take a look at what Jesus said to the invited guests. Jesus first deals with those who have already accepted the invitation and shown up.[15] While Luke calls this a parable, it reads more like an instruction set from Jesus on where to sit. Many might dismiss this as a trivial concern or an antiquated example of deferential social protocol. But for innovating it turns out to be as significant and substantive as it evidently was for Jesus.

Jesus said "when you are invited" (and show up), "sit down at the lowest place, so that when your host comes, he may say to you, 'Friend, move up higher.'" What does this have to do with anything besides showing a humble deference to the host? Does it have anything to do with responding to change or creating new value?

Innovating proves difficult for those in preferred seating. Incumbents are typically those who occupy and hold these seats. Success experienced by incumbents, however, proves to be the enemy of innovation. It works against creating new value for others. An incumbent perspective tends to "over-stand" rather than understand. To truly understand the new realities change brings, one must view these new realities from the ground up.

The trajectory of over-standing goes up and over. The trajectory for understanding goes down and under. True understanding is born out of humility and looking at the context from below. The truth of this has been expressed in various ways. For example, MIT social psychologist Edgar Schein calls this trajectory the unlearning that necessarily precedes the deep learning of something new.[16] More recently C. Otto Scharmer points to the "U" as the shape of the path anyone must traverse if authentic understanding is to be realized.[17] Only through humility can we start to appreciate and understand. Scharmer convincingly suggests that before one can make any sense of change or even hope to create new value in response to it, one must go deeper, even to the point of letting go much of what one thought was true. This resonates with what I believe Jesus intended when he said, "Truly I tell you, unless you change and become like children, you will never enter the kingdom of heaven."[18] It is also not unlike the way he concludes this parable in Luke: "For all who exalt themselves will be humbled, and those who humble themselves will be exalted."[19]

15. Luke 14:7–11.
16. Schein, "Anxiety of Learning."
17. Scharmer, *Theory U*, 27–47.
18. Matt 18:3.
19. Luke 14:11.

Habitual bias for preferred seating distorts perception and blocks understanding. It is natural to want to extend our incumbency. But this will turn the invitation of change back into an interruption. Change will appear either an inconvenient interruption or a threatening disruption. Incumbents are by definition those who have the luxury of not having to learn.[20] As for the Pharisees with whom Jesus was sharing the meal when he told this parable, preferred seating was difficult to give up. But it is precisely this kind of seating that prevents us from accepting change, responding to it, and effectively co-creating new value with the company of God.

HOSTS

Between the first and the third parable[21] Jesus turns his attention to the role of the host.[22] This could be a special word to leaders. In contexts of innovating these hosts are often called "sponsors"—executives with the power, authority and resources to provide safe haven for otherwise vulnerable early stage efforts aimed at creating new value.

In Luke's retelling of it, Jesus speaks directly to his host, a leader of the Pharisees.[23] Jesus offers what appears to be advice about who should be on the host's guest list. A closer reading reveals the concern is not just about *who*. It is really about *why*. Jesus is interested in a host's motivation. The concern is about conflicts of interest, even the appearance of a conflict. "Do not invite your friends or your brothers or your relatives or your rich neighbors, in case they may invite you in return and you would be repaid." Rather, invite those who *cannot* repay, Jesus tells his host, because "you will be repaid at the resurrection of the righteous."

The implication is as striking as it is challenging. From this point of view, giving more than receiving, or creating value more than extracting it, is the primary motivation for innovating. For commercial organizations there is certainly a practical requirement to make a profit from the innovating effort. For individuals we would want to experience some satisfaction for our sacrifices. However, when profit becomes confused with purpose,

20. Attributed to the late Czech social and political scientist Karl W. Deutsch.

21. The second parable on invitations in Luke 14:15–24 is not referred to explicitly as a parable and may indeed be an extension of the first parable. However, in v. 16 Jesus seem to be starting the second parable (see Bovon, *Luke 2*, 364).

22. Luke 14:12–14.

23. Luke 14:1.

innovating becomes harder to justify. When personal satisfaction becomes our interest, we can miss seeing and understanding what is of value to the other. Even change loses its invitational character. Transactions become more important than relationships and little if anything happens in creating new value. If new value is to be created, hosts must ask themselves why it should be created and why their organization is the one to attempt it. If intentions are to contribute—to give more than get—then the effort to create new value will likely be more aligned with the company of God.

When someone resolves to create value for another, initially the value being created is rarely clear, much less confirmed. The proposed value must be received and put to use by the one for whom the value is intended. It is essential to get an untested innovation into the hands of the one for whom it is designed. Experience "in use" precedes any trustworthy assignment of value. When the primary intentions are more about the expected return— what the innovator is going to get out of the deal—then a conflict of interest arises. The ensuing effort is suspect from the beginning. It becomes even more difficult to gain any experience for the untested innovation.

Early prototypes must be offered to customers to try out. These early prototypes are themselves invitational more than transactional. At this stage, the value being created has yet to be confirmed. The only way to confirm it is to invite those for whom the value is intended to try it out. If anything is sought "in return" it is the value of the potential relationship with the invitee and perhaps a chance to try again.

Evidence of positive and pure intent is inherent to the creative act, especially when the goal of what is being created is new value for another. Such creative effort does not happen out of transactions. It happens out of relationships—solid, trusting ones with plenty of mutual generosity and respect.

It is a bit surprising how many believe innovations emerge out of the transactional marketplace. They do not. Markets do not innovate, much less respond. Markets react. Markets also recognize and provide transactional access to new value to be sure. But the new value itself is created and nurtured elsewhere. It is this elsewhere that is often ignored even by those who are intent on extracting value from innovating.

Innovations always start with intentions that are more about what one can contribute than about what one can "get." An example can be found in what is still, despite some tough years, an icon of innovation, the Hewlett-Packard Company (HP). It was just this principle—contribution comes first, returns come later—that David Packard and Bill Hewlett turned into a regular practice in the early years of the company. Packard expressed it this way: "The key to HP's prospective involvement in any field is *contribution*. . . . We always asked, 'How can we make a contribution based on our strengths and our knowledge?' Then we'd ask, 'Who needs it?'"[24] The two founders of HP did not ask first what they would get from their effort. Rather, they asked themselves where they might be in a position to contribute value.[25]

The motivation of innovators should be on balance more about contributing, more about creating value, than on extracting returns. When leaders confuse profit with purpose, such confusion infects attitudes about change and disables efforts to create new value. This confusion happens often enough, frequently amplified by impatient time horizons and a surprising ignorance of the necessity for the "protected" space that caring and committed relationships require to nurture and raise an innovation.

This is a prime reason why innovation is so difficult for so many otherwise seemingly competent and able individuals and organizations. This is also where a theology of innovation should be able to make a significant contribution itself. Theology is deeply familiar with matters of greater purpose and relationships that serve no other purpose than the relationship itself. Transactional orientations can erode relationships built on love—both love of God and love of neighbor. This was a chronic problem recognized by the prophets.[26] And this will always be an issue when the question of value is center stage.

Theology is also familiar with the generative dynamics that animate a gift and the giving of it. Lewis Hyde looks at these dynamics in an economic context in his book *The Gift*.[27] Hyde's analysis affords a practical foil for an innovation theology to address the intersection of purpose, profits[28] and value creation. Hyde observes that a gift behaves differently than a commodity. The sale of a commodity turns a profit. Gifts do not *earn* profit so much as they "give increase."[29] The "vector of increase in a gift exchange stays in motion by following the [gift], while in commodity exchange the

---

24. Packard, *HP Way*, 96–97.

25. Ibid., 146.

26. Mic 6:6–8

27. Hyde, *The Gift*, 38–39.

28. Or outcomes from nonprofits.

29. Hyde, *The Gift*, 38–39.

increase stays behind as profit."[30] The grace (gifting) of God follows a relational logic, not a transactional one. The very value we attempt to create when we innovate is diminished by the sheer extraction of a portion of it for profit. Attempts to account for the value *before* it is created or confirmed often shut down innovating efforts before they get off the ground.

Many who attempt to innovate often completely miss this necessary and inconvenient truth. This is especially the case in commercial contexts where pressures are great to calculate imagined returns even before the reality of the value is confirmed. Calculating anticipated returns, and then believing the calculations, often kills attempts to create new value before they start. Prototypes are never put into the hands of those for whom they are intended. Invitations are never sent, hosts step back from being hosts at all. And we are left with transactions instead of relationships.

THE INVITED

Luke's third vignette[31] deals with those invited who have yet to show up. The invited are those in the "space" Viktor Frankl located as between stimulus and response wherein is "our power to choose."[32]

As the parable tells it, all of the invited declined. Each ends up making excuses as to why they chose not to accept. Each has more important matters to attend to, including matters of property, projects and personal relationships. These are incumbent matters. Accepting and showing up would be an interruption. Word gets back to the host that all declined and, understandably, the host is angry.

Then something striking happens in Luke's telling of it. A distinct shift in word choice alone sends the signal. Luke suddenly stops using "invite"[33]—a word Luke uses no less than ten times in ten prior verses.[34] When all have declined, the host stops inviting and starts enrolling, even compelling them to attend. The host has his servant *"bring in"* the poor, the crippled, the blind and the lame—those who not only cannot repay, but

30. Ibid.

31. Luke 14:15–24.

32. Frankl, *Man's Search for Meaning.*

33. Luke reserves one more use of invited (called) in his conclusion to the parable in v. 24 and this is to punctuate and contrast the consequences for those who were invited but refused.

34. Luke 14:7–17.

may have a harder time showing up on their own. These need assistance just to get themselves there. Even after these have been brought in, the host's house is still not filled. Here Luke uses the word "*compel*" to describe what the host will do to fulfill his plans and accomplish his goals.

This is the same word Paul used to describe the divine constraint he felt he was under.[35] It is the same word Aristotle used in his *Metaphysics*, meaning the force of "immanent necessity"—a condition that is essential (in Latin it is *conditio sine qua non*)—without which the event would not happen.[36] In the Old and New Testaments the word means "constraint."[37] In other words, change eventually constrains and compels as and when its original invitation is ignored or declined. Our response to it becomes a necessity and obligation, no longer the free, willing and voluntary response that was desired at first with the invitation.

Luke leaves us with an image of God's ever widening reach, a reach that is not thwarted by the lack of acceptance from those on the original guest list—those who declined. God's will in change "*will* be done," whether the invitation offered is accepted or not. Like spreading ripples on the surface of the water, the new is often rejected in its early form, often by the very entrenched and incumbent interests it was intended to serve. But eventually, unevenly to be sure, different forms of change (or innovation for that matter) show up in ever widening places, sometimes where least expected. This is a recognizable pattern in both change and innovation.

When change first becomes apparent we are invited to respond. The invitation may expire, but the change does not. It will eventually happen with or without us, regardless whether we accept or decline. Eventually change becomes impossible to resist, regardless of our efforts to ignore, delay or deny.

Invitations have time limits. Change does not. Change keeps moving. It does not wait. God still creates. When the invitation expires, unaccepted, it turns change from an invitation to an obligation, from an opportunity to create new value to a necessity to react to. As a necessity it forces adjustments and coping, which in turn leave us with little inclination or time to respond.

There are consequences to whether we respond to change and how. The consequences affect us more than they do the change itself. Any host

---

35. 1 Cor 9:16.

36. *TDNT*, s.v. "anake" (1:344).

37. Ibid.

would prefer the invited to accept. It's reasonable to assume that God also would prefer us to accept the invitation and show up and participate freely, willingly and under our own volition. However, whether we accept or not, the banquet will be held, the change will happen, with or without us.

Luke concludes the parable with a description that sounds very much like a prescription. It describes the consequences for those who decline. They do not get to taste the dinner. They do not get to participate, make a contribution, or even respond.

This extended parable in Luke seems to leave us with a choice. In our response to change, will we choose to be those who make it happen, those who let it happen or those who are left wondering what just happened?

5

Making Sense of Change

ACCEPTING CHANGE IS ONE thing. Reimaging it as an invitation is another. Making sense of it is still another. All three are prerequisites for responding to change, required for innovating, and engage the head and heart.

We may never fully accept change unless and until we make sense of it. Likewise, we may never really make enough sense of change until we accept it. The line where making sense starts and acceptance ends may not be so easy to draw.

The difficulty in drawing such a line comes in part from familiarity. Making sense is something most of us are doing all the time, whether we are conscious of it or not. More pronounced occasions of change may cause us to be more aware of our own sense-making, if only because we have to work harder at it. But even on these occasions we are unlikely to pay much attention to *how* we make sense of change. Like the sawyer with too much work, it is difficult to take time out to sharpen the saw. Sharpening the saw of sense-making is what this chapter is about.

Because making sense is so second nature to us, it makes sense here to clarify what sense-making is and is not. An example is always helpful.

In August of 1966, a friend and colleague, Dr. Stuart Brown, was enjoying his new status as an assistant professor of psychiatry at Baylor University. A call came to him from Texas Governor John Connolly. The governor was requesting a full investigation into what quickly came to be known as the Texas Tower Massacre.

Charles Whitman had just ascended the tower at the University of Texas in Austin, killing fifteen and wounding thirty-one before being gunned down by an off-duty police officer and a courageous citizen. Even before Whitman climbed the tower he had killed his wife and mother. Seventeen dead. Over thirty wounded. Few of Whitman's victims knew him and even fewer were known by him.

Connolly wanted to make sense of this senseless event. How many others like Whitman were out there? Could anything be done to prevent this in the future? Stuart took charge of the psychiatric evaluation of Whitman, perhaps the most crucial part of the investigation—a formal and well-funded sense-making effort.

When the investigation began, most speculated Whitman was a raving, deranged and paranoid maniac. But a surprisingly different picture emerged from extensive interviews with people who knew Whitman. He turned out to be a "seemingly loving husband and son; an ex-Marine, who had been the youngest Eagle Scout in the history of the Boy Scouts."[1] The normal, achieving, even impressive image in the foreground was shadowed by a background of an over-controlling father who incessantly abused Whitman's mother, along with a barely noticed but surprisingly lifelong pattern, or absence of one: Charles Whitman never played.

Stuart confessed to me that at first he really didn't think much of Whitman's own absence of play. It was a minor note in the report to Connelly. But when other studies of dark and nefarious cases came to Stuart for investigation—a dubious result of the notoriety of this case—he began to notice a recurring pattern. The pattern has now come to be called "play deprivation." What Stuart first saw in Whitman's background showed up in the psychiatric evaluations of others whose crimes were as heinous as the resulting carnage was tragic. Since the confirmation of this pattern, Stuart has given the better part of his professional career to tracking the evidentiary science behind play.[2]

What makes Stuart's experience such a good example of sense-making is the presence and sequence of several factors.[3] First, someone noticed something that no one else had noticed. It is at first *noticed* as something that doesn't quite fit—something that stands out in contrast to the flow of things. In this case it was the absence of play. Second, what was noticed

1. Brown, *Play*, 94.
2. See the National Institute for Play website (nifplay.org).
3. Weick, *Sensemaking in Organizations*, 2.

becomes *noted*. The note is published or made available to a broader community, allowing what one person notes to be noticed by others. Third, there was some *delay* before others actually start to notice what was noted. Even Stuart himself did not pay as much attention at first to what he noted in Whitman's evaluation, at least not until he started noticing a similar pattern in other cases. Such delays arise because experts tend to overestimate "the likelihood that they would surely know about the phenomenon if it actually were taking place."[4] Which leads to a fourth factor in the sense-making sequence: how *identity and reputation* of the one who is doing the noticing and noting affects how the sense is made.

The sense we make of change is often questioned or rejected by the one who makes the first sense to begin with. Experts learn to keep to themselves the first sense they make. This is due to the near universal experience of encountering events that at first seemed so implausible most of us hesitate to report it for fear we will not be believed. "Because I don't know about it, it must not be going on." The hesitation "not only discourages curiosity . . . but also frequently creates an antagonistic stance" toward the newly noted.[5] This self-imposed silence constrains and delays the sharing and ultimate validation of the sense made. Identity, reputation and even parochial interests appear to get in the way of making a sense that can benefit others.

While Stuart's experience is dramatic, all of us have our own bank of sense-making experiences. Some of those experiences come from making sense of the movements and contrasts that interrupt the continuity and flow of our lives. Some of these movements and contrasts we would call life changing. Others might be merely bumps on the road or potholes in our way. Some changes are harder to make sense of than others. As we get older we accumulate more sense-making experience and we become more aware of just how much we don't know. At the same time we can become more tolerant of the imprecision of the sense we *can* make, and the perfect sense that we cannot.

Our own interests, identity and biases shape the sense we make for ourselves, even when it makes little or no sense for the other. Likewise, what makes sense to the other may not make complete sense to us. But if we are to create new value for another, we can only succeed when we see both sense and value made, and the other sees it too.

4. Ibid.

5. Ibid.

Typically the sense we make of change we make for ourselves first. When we do, the sense we make is about orienting or reorienting the way we see and understand the world, in light of what just changed. Making sense of change for others, however, requires us to express and embody the sense we make in what the other finds valuable.

When we make sense without the company of God—without a theological perspective—the sense we make may have a shorter shelf life and be of less value. It's likely to make any related innovating effort more challenging than it already is and innovating is surely challenging enough as it is. Making sense of change in the company of God, however, can make all the difference in the world, not only for the other, but for ourselves as well.

SENSE-MAKING

Interpreting is not sense-making. Sense-making surely *includes* interpreting but is not the same. What is interpreted is typically a static text or spoken word. In contrast, making sense has us confronting dynamic, ambiguous contexts with ill-defined boundaries. Creative poking and prodding are called for. An interpreter's detached and objective view is necessary but insufficient. Probing the environment around us—the living contexts that we want to make sense of—produces feedback and this feedback tells us something fresh, real and trustworthy. It gives us direct experience with which to learn more about how our environment responds.

Interpreting concentrates on discovery and an accurate and complete diagnosis. In contrast, sense-making includes both invention and discovery—inventing the probes and discovering what the context "says" back to us when it is probed. Those who study sense-making suggest that when trying to make sense of change we are typically more interested in effective engagement than accurate assessment, timely response more than thorough analysis, and even creating new value for others more than ensuring objective diagnosis of the situation.

Making sense of change is never confined to cool cognition. Emotions and memories affect and infect the entire sense-making process. This is especially the case when someone or something precious to us is at stake. From sensors that receive the signals to the interpretive cognitive processing mechanisms embedded in our thinking, even to the way we form the meaning we "make," sense-making is an open, complex and dynamic process, vulnerable to all sorts of missed signals, distortions, misinterpretations and misunderstandings.

The perceptual, cognitive, affective and memory mechanisms involved in our individual sense-making comprise a complex tangle of interwoven and iterating sensors, processors, memories and feedback loops. The sense we make is really revealed, discovered, and invented as much as it is made. For an individual, the sense-making system may be more neurological, though it is not without a social dimension. For an organization, the system may be more social, though it is not without cognitive and affective dimensions.

Several factors set sense-making apart from other ways of explaining things, like understanding, interpretation and attribution,[6] partly because sense-making is not done in the abstract. Rather it happens within our identities, our near term projects and the broader narratives of which we are a part.

Identity. Sense-making is constrained by the sense-maker's own sense of self. Who we imagine ourselves to be and where we are—in life, in career, in some imagined pecking order—will influence what we sense and notice to begin with.

I learned this early in my experience facilitating small groups of scientists and engineers called together for problem-solving and invention. Collaborative problem-solving is not just about finding inventive solutions together. It's also about making sense together. While the explicit purpose of each meeting was to solve whatever the stated problem was, there were always other "agendas." Part of the job of a facilitator is to make sure these other agendas don't divert energy and focus from the stated purpose which these other agendas have a way of doing.

Anticipating these other agendas is impossible. There are simply too many of them, and too much variety, complexity and transience to make it worth giving any of these agendas any attention at all, except for one. The one exception turns out to be the same for every individual at every meeting, regardless of the individual. It's an agenda that accompanies each of us all the time: to establish, build or maintain self-esteem. It is a very safe bet that this agenda is current and active for every person, always. Should this identity agenda in any way be threatened, it can sabotage the stated purpose.

---

6. Ibid., 17. Weick names seven factors—identity, retrospect, enactment, social, ongoing, extracted cues, and plausibility. I have condensed his list down to three for the sake of brevity and, of course, for the sense I am attempting to make.

As a result, I learned subtle and efficient ways to attend to these identity agendas for each individual: giving him credit for whatever contribution was made, or writing up her idea in words that she used, or acknowledging each by name. Rarely did I ever encounter individuals whose identity needs exceeded the attention deposits I could give. When identity needs are quiet, there is less noise from within to interfere with a full-bodied attention to the task at hand. But when worried about establishing, maintaining or building our identity, individually or organizationally, the worry is likely to interfere with the clarity of perception and reception of the signals change is sending.

Identity influences the sense we make and how we make it and the very things we sense to begin with. If identity is in crisis or threatened in any way, it will distort the field of our perceiving. A still,[7] secure and quiet identity is unlikely to interfere, deny or even delude the sense-making effort.

Current Projects. Most of us are always in the middle of things, and the things with the middles we are in are our projects. When change muddles these middles we instinctually use our current projects to help us make sense.

When change comes, among the first questions asked is whether the change or any part of it is relevant. "Does it matter?" Does this change threaten a delay or serendipitously advance the cause of any of our projects? Our criterion of relevance has more to do with what's on our plate than with the new realities emerging in the change. If we cannot see and find a way to do something about the change in the context of our current projects, then we are more likely to ignore it than try to make sense of it.

To a large extent our current projects determine what is relevant to us. Our projects—individually and collectively—filter what is signal from what is just noise. These filters are also woven with the threads of our experience and expertise. What we imagine is relevant helps us filter *out* what we can ignore and filter *in* what we can use. Relevancy is partly a function of our current set of projects and partly a function of our previous experience and accumulated knowledge. In short, our current projects, experience and knowledge define what is relevant and calibrate the porosity of our filters.

Most of us have more than one project on our plates, not to mention a variety of different experiences and knowledge bases upon which to draw. This variety and plurality is both good news and bad news. The good news is that we have a rich and robust set of experiences, knowledge and projects we will use to make sense of any change we encounter. The bad news is that there are many possible meanings that can be "made," depending upon the

---

7. Ps 46:10.

variety of projects on our plate and the experience banks from which we choose to draw.

Ambiguity is the real challenge here, more than uncertainty, especially when we make sense of change. The irony here is how often we think we need more information when we are trying to make sense of change. What we really need is clarity more than certainty. Uncertainty is a problem that is solved with more and better information. Ambiguity and confusion are problems solved with greater clarity. What is needed when change overwhelms and confuses is not more information. What is needed is clarity about preferences to help the sense-maker determine what matters.[8] Our current projects, along with our past experiences and accumulated knowledge can help address the ambiguity and even the uncertainty challenge. But our projects, experiences and knowledge will always remain a limiter.

Longer-term Narrative. Our longer-term aspirations are another influence on how we make sense of change. One of the first things we ask is whether the change is more threat or opportunity. Answers will depend largely on how the change intersects with our longer-term goals and directions, or perhaps more importantly, how it advances or hinders our progress in the narrative flow and direction of our lives. This is the case for both individuals and organizations.

Retrospective and prospective views play into how we make meaning in the present. Having a sense of where we have been and where we are headed gives us a narrative within which to make sense of what just happened, whatever it is, and whether it is relevant or not. The plots and sub-plots of our individual unfolding narratives help us locate ourselves and understand the present, especially when change appears without sense or warning.

In this context, interestingly enough, it is plausibility even more than accuracy (and verifiability) that contributes more to the sense we try to make. Karl Weick puts it this way:

> In an equivocal, postmodern world, infused with the politics of interpretation and conflicting interests, and inhabited by people with multiple shifting identities, an obsession with accuracy seems fruitless, and not of much practical help, either. Of much more help are myths, metaphors, fables, epics and paradigms. Each of these resources contains a good story . . . [and stories] explain [and] energize.[9]

8. Weick, *Sensemaking in Organizations*, 27–28.
9. Ibid., 61.

MAKING SENSE IN THE COMPANY OF GOD

Theology deals in stories that explain and energize. In fact, it is the very purpose of theology to make sense of the stories we are living, not just to explain but also to energize, not just to bring understanding, but also hope. Theology contributes to the way we make sense by bringing a transcendent, deeper or greater purpose to all three of these sense-making factors—our identity, our current projects and our longer-term narrative.

Theology can quiet the needs of our identities and reminds us that we are creatures of the Creator's making, beloved children of our Heavenly Father, and servants of a company and mission that is greater than our own, as the servant songs in Isaiah so potently remind us.[10] In regards to our current projects, theology assumes the potential in each of these projects, no matter how seemingly mundane or secular. Everyday projects can be the carriers of what Paul Tillich calls our ultimate concern, however partial.[11] And in regards to our long-term narrative, theology invites us to see ourselves as participants in an ongoing and larger narrative of the company of God.

Without a theological perspective, making sense will be more difficult, gaining clarity more vulnerable to the quest for more data, and filtering out the noise more challenging. Theology may be essential to sense-making in general, and especially useful in making sense of change.

Like theology, innovating itself is also an act of sense-making, especially in regards to change. Change was central to what management thinker Peter Drucker described as essential to innovators. These entrepreneurial people are

> not content simply to improve on what already exists, or to modify it. They try to create new and different values and new and different satisfactions, to convert a "material" into a "resource," or to combine existing resources in a new and more productive configuration. And it is change that always provides the opportunity for the new and different. *Systematic innovation therefore consists in the purposeful and organized search for changes, and in the systematic analysis of the opportunities such changes might offer for economic or social innovation.*[12]

---

10. Isa 42:1–9; 49:1–12; 50:4–9; 52:13—53:12.

11. Tillich, *Systematic Theology*, 1:13.

12. Drucker, *Innovation and Entrepreneurship*, 34–35 (italics in original).

Both innovating and theology are essentially sense-making efforts. Combining them into an integrated effort seems like a reasonable, if not practical, thing to do. Such combination and integration might take the best sense-making practices from both in order to find better ways of making sense of change and creating new value for others than either one could do on its own.

MORE THAN PROCESSED INFORMATION

Even without an explicit theological perspective, many continue to describe how we make sense using an information-processing metaphor. Such a model assumes that we first sense what is going on around us, and even within us, from a diverse array of sensors—eyes, ears, nose, tongue and tactile nerve endings distributed throughout our bodies. Then we process the electrochemical signals these distributed sensors deliver to the brain, sometimes consciously, sometimes not. This processing many call cognition, which is not only affected by the signals it receives from sensors, but also from stored signals that come from memory, hence recognition.

Using the operations of a computer to characterize how we make sense is understandable. The dominant imagination can't help but be influenced by the pervasiveness of computational devices and repeated declarations that we are living in the information age and operating in the knowledge economy. Digital choreographies of electrons do show some analogous affinities for the electrochemical firings of synaptic structures in our brains.

However well it works as a metaphor though, it just doesn't sound all that plausible. The realities of how we make sense are more open-ended, social and organic than the rather closed, individual and deterministic processes programmed in computers. Describing what happens in our brains when we make sense as information-processing is seductively familiar but intuitively troubling, and quite possibly dangerously inaccurate.

The information-processing analogy breaks down like other mismatches between the metaphors we use to name complex systems and the nature of those systems. The metaphors may be familiar but they don't quite fit. Russell Ackoff points to these mismatches as seductively misleading classifications. For Ackoff the critical variable for classification is choice,[13] a variable that is

---

13. Ackoff, *Re-Creating the Corporation*, 21.

particularly relevant in making sense of change. Theology can help us understand and even clarify the importance of choice in making sense.[14]

Ackoff suggests four types of systems, classified by where choice shows up within these systems. The four he names as deterministic, animated, social and ecological. A system that has no choice, either in its constituent parts or as a whole—like automobiles, fans, and clocks—is *deterministic*. A system wherein the parts have no choice but the whole does—animals, humans and other living organisms—is an *animated* system. Systems that have the capability of choice in both parts and as a whole—like organizations, communities or whole societies—these are *social* systems. And finally, systems where the parts are capable of choice but the whole cannot choose, these systems are ecologies or *ecosystems*.

When we use a deterministic metaphor (e.g., computer) to describe an animated system (e.g., sense-making) we mismatch the metaphor with the reality it is intended to describe. These mismatches produce less than desirable results.[15] The way we make sense as an individual—to the extent that we really make sense alone—is more of an animated system than it is deterministic. The way we make sense as an organization is more of a social system than it is deterministic.

The information-processing metaphor for sense-making assumes not only that there is sense to be made from the information processed. It also assumes that what is meant by information is commonly understood. Both of these assumptions simply don't bear the weight of closer examination.

Look more closely at what is meant by information. In the late 1980s Milan Zeleny and Russell Ackoff contributed to what has now become a standard way of differentiating data, information, knowledge, understanding and wisdom.[16] It is commonly referred to as the "information hierarchy." All levels of the hierarchy are involved in making sense.

Twenty years after Ackoff's earliest version of the hierarchy he reexpressed his original with characteristic clarity. Here is how he described the hierarchy:

> There are five types of content in the human mind: data, information, knowledge, understanding, and wisdom. They form a hierarchy: information is more valuable than data, knowledge more valuable than information, understanding more valuable than

14. Moser, *Elusive God*, 55–60.

15. Ibid., 30.

16. See Ackoff, "From Data to Wisdom"; and Zeleny, "Management Support Systems."

knowledge, and wisdom more valuable than understanding. Nevertheless schools and organizations of all types tend to focus on the lower-valued aspects of mental content (especially information) rather than on the more highly valued understanding and wisdom.

Data consists of symbols that represent properties of objects and events. For example, street addresses designate locations using numeric and alphabetic symbols. Inventories consist of numbers attached to various items identified alphabetically. These too are data.

Information consists of data that have been processed to be useful. They are related much as iron ore is to iron. Very little can be done with iron ore (data) but once it is converted to iron (information) it has very many uses. Information is contained in descriptions, answers to questions that begin with words such as who, what, when, and how many.

Knowledge as know-how is contained in instructions, answers to questions that begin with "how to." It is one thing to know in what city some activity is located—information—but another to know how to get there—knowledge. It is one thing to know that an automobile can carry you from one place to another—information—but another to know how to get there—knowledge.

It is yet another matter to know why a person wants to go there. Explanations are contained in answers to questions beginning with why. They provide *understanding*.

Data, information, knowledge, and understanding all can contribute to the efficiency with which we can pursue objectives; with whether we do things right.

Wisdom, on the other hand, is concerned with effectiveness, whether we do the right thing. Wisdom is contained in evaluations. It provides a person with a willingness to make short-term sacrifices in order to make longer-term gains.

There is a significant difference between doing something right and doing the right things. The more efficiently we do the wrong thing, the "wronger" we become. When we correct an error committed in pursuing the wrong thing, we become "wronger." If we commit an error doing the right things and correct it we become "righter." Therefore, it is better to do the right thing wrong and correct it than to do the wrong thing right.[17]

Outside the company of God, without a theological perspective this hierarchy is left unframed. *In* the company of God the hierarchy is framed

17. Ackoff, *Differences*, 54–55.

with and by the purposes of God and the recognition of our own limitations. The Apostle Paul made this observation so concisely and beautifully in his first letter to the Corinthians.[18]

In a mere thirteen verses Paul frames what we in the information age and knowledge economy so often leave unframed. Paul frames it with the purposes of the company of God—to love—and with the reminder that all our data, information, knowledge, understanding and wisdom is partial and incomplete. In fact, even our sensing is "in a mirror," not a window. We are constantly distracted by the reflection of our own image, our own interests and our own identities. And not only is it a mirror, it is "dim." In the Greek the word "dimly" actually means riddle. The English word for it is enigma—"a perplexing mysterious, or unexplained thing."[19]

Early in his first letter to the church in Corinth Paul takes on both the top and the bottom of this information hierarchy. Paul says that some—the Greeks—desire wisdom while others—the Jews—desire data.[20] But both wisdom and data, and all that is in between, are framed by the wisdom of God at the top and bottom of the frame. The enigma[21] in the center of the frame is the mysterious reality of the sense made in Christ crucified. This center is a "stumbling block" and "foolishness" to those who place their bets on data and human wisdom, whose information hierarchy is left theologically unframed.

This is not to imply that content up and down the information hierarchy is senseless and without value. It is to say, however, that what we know and understand, and the data and information that feeds both, is always partial and incomplete. It is also to say that when our incomplete understanding and wisdom is framed by the purposes of the company of God, this incompleteness is not the handicap it is when we try to make sense without a theological perspective, especially when aiming to create new value for others.

NOT JUST IN THE BRAIN

Many cognitive scientists assume that the brain is where all the "processing" or sense-making occurs. "Cephalocentric" is what neurologist Frank

---

18. 1 Cor 13.

19. *New Shorter Oxford English Dictionary*, s.v. "enigma."

20. 1 Cor 1:22.

21. Wink, *Human Being*, 19–34.

Wilson calls this prevalent but mistaken assumption.[22] Wilson makes a persuasive case for a more distributed sense-making. Wilson contends that not only the hands but the whole body is engaged in making sense. It doesn't all happen in the brain.

Making sense is not merely some cognitive processing function that occurs in cortical matter where data-feeds are processed, inputs from sensors are compared with retrieved patterns stored in memory, and thought outputs are produced. Rather:

> both the desire and the capacity to learn are present in all of us, and both are difficult (though not impossible) to extinguish. Both grow, take shape, and continually reinforce one another through the action of the many seen and unseen hands that will touch us, move us, guide us, challenge us, and protect us for as long as we live. The desire to learn is reshaped continuously as brain and hand vitalize one another, and the capacity to learn grows continuously as we fashion our own personal laboratory for making things,[23]

and for making sense as well; with brains, yes; but also, hands; ours, others and God's.

Wilson and others[24] will not let us rest comfortably imagining that we make sense like computers process information. The image of the detached, objective scientist, while potent and pervasive, is no longer tenable either as description or prescription for making sense.[25]

Making sense is in the *making*. This is not confined to cognitive processing in the brain but involves where and how we interact, engage and "interface" (to borrow a word from systems thinking) with the social and physical world around us. We may be able to imagine ourselves as distinct and detached individuals. But while we may be able to imagine this, reality will not let us escape being a participant in our particular social and physical environments.

22. Wilson, *Hand*, 295 ("sense-making" added).

23. Ibid.

24. Weick, *Sensemaking in Organizations*, 44.

25. The Heisenberg uncertainty principle in quantum mechanics and the related observer effects in physics no longer allow us the option of being "uninvolved." In 1927 Werner Heisenberg first proposed (and it was subsequently confirmed) that there is a fundamental limit to the precision with which certain pairs of simultaneous physical properties at the quantum level can be known. What Heisenberg proposed for quantum dynamics was an observer effect that also applies to other areas of physics—that the observer alters what is observed.

Theology has known this for sometime. It's in the truth of what's called the *imago Dei*—the image of God. We first encounter the *imago Dei* very early in Scripture. In the first chapter of the first book it shows up as a foundational assumption of sorts. We are made in the image of God. And the only image of God we have at that point in Scripture comes from the previous twenty-five verses. The image is of a God who creates and makes, including making sense. If we are made in God's image, then we too are not only God's creations—God's creatures. We are creators ourselves, or at least co-creators. This image of God is an inescapable characteristic of who we are.

We create. We make sense, sometimes well and sometimes poorly. We do this in the *making*, whether it is making the sense we are able to make, or in enacting and forming that sense in relationships, products, policy, processes or problems solved. This is not only what we do. It is who we are.

This starting assumption may itself prove to be central to innovation theology. In fact, it may turn out to be what living a meaningful life requires of us—creating new value for others. If so, this implies that innovating is not some optional activity, but an essential act of living a life of meaning and purpose.

If there is any element of truth to this, then the sense we make about sense-making itself will recognize the inescapability of our entanglement with our own environment. This is a difficult thing for those of us who have grown up in what is an individualistic and self-centered culture. Imaging ourselves not as the center of our own lives but non-centric parts of a wider social and physical fabric doesn't come easily to us. Thinking of ourselves as supporting cast members rather than the central character feels strange. However, it is likely closer to the truth of the social and physical fabric of reality itself. It is certainly more aligned with a theological perspective.

A MODEL

When we make sense of change the sense we make will remain significantly handicapped without the influence of a theological perspective. As a result, a model is in order.

First, projecting sense-making on the "bigger screen" of how organizations make sense can help us visualize sense-making better than what may happen inside an individual where sense-making is more compact, integrated and autonomic. Such a projection also accounts for the social influences that are undoubtedly at work. The model comes from my experience with organizations' attempts to not only make sense of external changes but to convert the sense made into new value for others.

Picture three interoperating subsystems—sensing, interpreting and remembering—along with an ample set of feedback loops that enable these subsystems to interoperate. Many organizations have some form of these capabilities, often implicit and ungoverned. But whether explicitly managed or not, these capabilities directly influence the adaptive capability of the organization to respond to its external environment.

Sensing. Having multiple and varied sensors is essential. In an organization these sensors are people (not so much devices), each attuned to different interests, sources and frequencies. People who are naturally forward thinkers[26] may have their own way of taking in information, the most classic and well-known classification for which may be the Myers-Briggs Type Indicator. A variety of sensors brings robustness to an organization's ability to sense its environment. Who these forward thinkers are is very important. Not everyone is. The mix can be deliberately balanced or biased, depending upon the inclinations of the organization.

For example, if the immediate task is to overcome the organization's own blind spots or identify threats or opportunities, then diversity is essential. On the other hand, if the task is more oriented to preempting an organization's own autoimmune responses to change, then a sufficient representation of senior executives and resource stewards among the forward thinkers will be important.

Interpreting. Having some kind of mechanism that periodically brings inside what is sensed on the outside is necessary. Bringing outside forward thinkers together to creatively and collaboratively make sense goes a long way toward reducing perceived ambiguities, if not uncertainties. The results of such conversational collaborations are both interpretive *and* generative. These collaborations produce both shared meaning and common commitment in response to change. Conversations like these, whether formal or informal, turn out to be essential for creating new value. The sense made often describes both the foreground and the background—the context from which value (text) derives.

---

26. David Kelley, Founder of the design firm IDEO, refers to these people as "T" types: individuals who have, because of their position, experience or both, a broad perspective and an ability to go deep into the details of at least one relevant speciality.

While the metaphor of central processing may be useful to describe this interpreting subsystem, it is too computational. Rigorous analysis should be included in this interpreting, to be sure. But by no means should it be left to analysis alone. Analytical, interpretive *and* generative thinking are essential. This is why a computational (information processing) model misses the point. Sense-making can certainly start with observations which lead to discovery. However, sense-making must also engage in invention. Both discovery and invention are essential to making sense.

Remembering. What is remembered and how it is remembered is essential to making sense as well. What an organization remembers will significantly influence the sense it makes but also what it senses to begin with. The organization's memory may itself be comprised of three different types: traditional, short-term and future. Think of these as different types of pattern banks.

Traditional memory stores all types of routines and knowledge bases that could be regarded as important parts of the organization's intellectual assets. Like the autonomic memory in a human, what is in this memory is well known and understood by years of repeated experience. This memory can produce orthodoxies and filters that prevent new signals from even being recognized as signals. However, there is much knowledge contained in this kind of memory as well.

In *short-term memory* are recent experiences the organization has that have been formally reviewed for lessons learned. There is also likely much tacit knowledge adjacent to short-term memory that could be converted into an explicit form and included in this short-term memory. Often the contents of this memory include recent successes and failures and even hypotheses regarding the root causes.

In *future memory* are scenarios—narratives that are plausible and provocative—of what may and could occur but has not yet happened. These scenarios represent glimpses into the external landscape of the organization's future that differ from the organization's projected trajectory. Without this third type of memory the other two will eventually turn core capabilities into core rigidities.[27]

Recognition operates with all three of these memories and plays a special role for enabling sensing, interpreting and remembering to interoperate effectively. It is by recognizing not only past but also future patterns that

27. Leonard-Barton, "Core Capabilities and Core Rigidities," 111–25.

sensors (people) are encouraged to attend to what they might otherwise regard as noise without the pattern having been explicitly expressed.[28]

For recognition, Karl Weick speaks about what he calls "minimal sensible structures." These are many and varied but each provides a past frame into which we naturally and often unconsciously place cues from our present experience.[29] Meaning is made when we are able to construct a relation between a frame we have used in the past and a cue we experience in the present. This is what "connecting the dots" means.

Frames have their own vocabularies. These vocabularies name cues arising in our current experience. According to Weick, types of frames include vocabularies of society (ideologies), of organizations (operating assumptions or givens), of work (paradigms), of coping (theories of action), of predecessors (tradition) and of sequence and experience (stories).

Theology offers a rich set of minimal sensible structures for our sense-making. We need look no further than the stories, images, parables, poetry and songs of Scripture. Look deeper, however, and a theological perspective may offer even more than some additional sense-making structures. Given how theology incorporates not only tradition and story but also ideologies, assumptions, paradigms and theories of action, theology offers "master" minimal sensible structures. I don't believe it an exaggeration to say that, for Christians the gospel narrative is *the* sense maker. It has the ability to help us describe and prescribe or to frame, if you will, our present experience of change. It offers us ways to make sense that are perhaps more robust than any other minimal sensible structure alone.

A theological perspective, however, can become a closed conformance to orthodoxy rather than an open appreciation of what is experienced. When this happens, theology loses whatever humility it might have had, and the truth becomes a fixed proposition without life. In these instances, the vocabulary of the frame excludes rather than includes, narrows rather than expands, and constrains rather than liberates, the sense-maker. We force-fit the new realities of change into black-and-white distinctions that preserve the frame more than accept and appreciate the reality experienced. This turns sense-making into control taking. And it seldom works for very long, especially with change and innovation.

---

28. A prototypical story of Royal Dutch Shell's scenario-enabled ability to anticipate OPEC before any of the other oil companies illustrates the practical benefit of scenarios. See also, Schwartz, *Art of the Long View*, 53–56.

29. Weick, *Sensemaking in Organizations*, 111.

Despite this risk, sense-making with a theological perspective is more practical and encouraging than without one. With a theological perspective our identity needs, the demands of our current projects, and the continuity of our own narratives relax their collective grip on what is relevant. Something, or more properly some One, has taken their place.

In the company of God the need to establish, build and maintain our individual and social identities already has been satisfied. In the company of God we already have an identity—we are beloved children and voluntary servants. Anything else related to who we are is merely interesting, not essential. In the company of God our current projects themselves are no longer just *our* projects. They are projects of a company. If we sense that one or more of those projects doesn't seem to fit in the company of God, then such a project may be a candidate for termination or dissolution.

In the company God, our own narrative is really only meaningful in the context of the greater narrative of the company. There are not only others but the Other participating and contributing with us in the progress and completion of these projects. It is not up to us alone. As a participant and contributor to that narrative, we no longer need to be anxious.[30] Without these identity needs, misaligned projects, and independent narratives all clamoring for our attention, the sense we make of change is less apt to be distorted. We are freed to sense and appreciate the new realities of change on its own terms, not ours.

Some might imagine that such a perspective would narrow our choices and restrain our thinking. Quite the contrary, a theological perspective will not constrain us. When in the company of God we are freer— "emancipated" to use Walter Brueggemann's term[31]—to sense, interpret, and remember with less distortion from the needs of our own identity, the demands of our own projects, and the leading roles in our own narratives. We are instead liberated to sense what is real, to interpret what is true and to appreciate where we might contribute in supporting the larger, broader and deeper narrative beyond our parochial interests.

When our identity needs have already been met as children in, servants of, and heirs to, the company of God, we are freed from needs for attention, credit or acclaim. Such needs skew our sensing, interpreting and remembering. With conscious confidence in the projects in which we are engaged, we are freed to give it our all—whatever the project—because we believe these projects are contributing to a greater purpose.

30. Matt 6:24–34.
31. Brueggemann, *Practice of Prophetic Imagination*, 21–24.

Of course, this is all well and good in theory. Putting it into practice is an imperfect, two-steps-forward-one-step-back kind of experience. Turning toward and tuning in to that which we give our attention requires turning away from and tuning out the rest. This is especially the case when there is so much vying for our attention. According to some, the most important function of attention is our ability to screen out rather than take in.[32] How do we choose what and who to tune out? How do we know what is and is not relevant, especially when responding to change?

In the company of God, sensing the movements and contrasts in change become less the quick and anxious classification of "friend" or "foe" and more a seeking of what rings true, appears beautiful, and proves loving. Where we direct our eyes, ears, taste, touch and smell is not toward what satisfies our aesthetic sensibilities, appetites for personal satisfaction, or longing for our own comfort and security. Rather, our senses tune in to where there is hatred, injury, doubt, despair, darkness, and sadness as the company's purpose is to sow love, forgiveness, faith, hope, light, and joy.[33] In the company of God, interpreting is less about gaining control of the situation or insulating ourselves from it, and more about consoling, understanding and loving, certainly more than being consoled, understood or loved. And in our remembering in the company of God, we are more likely to find meaning and purpose when we forget ourselves, more likely to forgive when we know what it feels like to be forgiven, and more likely to awaken to a new life when we have experienced the death of our old selves.

Making sense is one thing. Making money is another, though the two often become intertwined in practice. This difference and intertwining is the subject of the next chapter.

32. Davenport and Beck, *Attention Economy*, 58.
33. From the St. Francis Prayer.

6

Make Meaning *Before* Money

FOUR YEARS AFTER THE dotcom bubble burst the entrepreneur and start-up investor Guy Kawasaki found himself speaking to an audience gathered by the Stanford Technology Ventures Program. He told them to make meaning before making money.[1]

Kawasaki explained, "If you make meaning you will probably make money. But if you set out to make money, chances are you will neither make money nor meaning." Kawasaki went on to situate meaning in one or more of the following: increase the quality of life for others, right a wrong, or prevent the end of something good. If the entrepreneurial effort does not have something to do with at least one of these, then perhaps the entrepreneur should reconsider.

Absence of meaning surely contributed to a few burst bubbles and foreshadowed Kawasaki's counsel. Though it may not always be followed, the advice reflects a growing desire on the part of many to do well by doing good. Social venturing, B-corporations, and even many for-profit ventures express interest in both cause *and* commercial success.

Lack of meaning is not the only cause of punctured bubbles. It is also the lack of value, perhaps even more so. The products and services many dotcom companies envisioned left promised value unrealized. As much "vaporware" as software was developed, due in part to what Gartner,

---

1. Guy Kawasaki, "Make Meaning in Your Company," Stanford Technology Ventures Program Educators Corner, School of Engineering, Stanford University, October 20, 2004, https://www.youtube.com/watch?v=lQs6IpJQWXc.

Inc. now regularly tracks and calls the hype cycle.[2] Hype cycles continue to demonstrate that meaning is often *conceived* before any money is really made.[3] Value can never be created without a customer, client or beneficiary recognizing and validating it by the exchange of their cash or by the outcomes achieved for the cause.

Kawasaki is right, but only partly. Both meaning *and* value are at the heart of making sense of change. In the process, however, we can end up either creating meaning without value, or creating value without meaning.

Meaning made *without value* ends up being a private matter. Certainly I can make sense of change for myself only. Personal meaning may improve my ability to navigate in a chaotic and nonsensical world, or it helps me to get along with others. But it remains psychological or emotional, confined to private and personal realms. It lacks public or shared value. When private meaning trumps public value, people isolate and insulate themselves. And when making money for ourselves trumps the making of meaning and value for others, the future of the other is sacrificed at the altar of our own individual interests. Sooner or later, however, our own private interests prove parochial, insufficient and of limited meaning, particularly when compared to the greater meaning and purpose found in creating value for others.

Value *without meaning*, on the other hand, confines value to a financial frame. Money may be made to be sure, but whether meaning and value accompany this money-making may not be so obvious. When money is made without meaning, both our understanding of value and efforts to create it remain merely acquisitive, transactional, and closely associated with only what can be quantified, measured and monetized.

Making money is more a *result* than purpose of any commercial enterprise.[4] Failure to distinguish between result and purpose continues to lead many astray. In fact, when pursuit of financial performance comes at the expense of purpose, it can be an early indicator of the decline to come.[5]

The following looks at what a theological perspective brings to meaning, value and money and how each influences the other. It is especially interested in the *making* of each, given how often money overshadows the other two. Bringing a theological perspective to our understanding

2. "Hype Cycle" is a branded graphical presentation used by the Gartner Group—an information technology research and advisory group.

3. "Making money" should not to be confused with receiving investors' money.

4. Drucker, *Management*, 60, 61.

5. Collins, *How the Mighty Fall*, 54.

of meaning, value and money reintegrates an understanding of value that all too often becomes disintegrated, delaminated and compartmentalized. Theology offers perhaps the best means for us to return to a more holistic notion of value—an integrated view that is not possible through economics, ethics, or their combination alone.

Said differently, making sense of change and creating new value for others relies to a great extent on connecting dots in the company of God. We are more likely to select substantive dots to connect and connect them in ways that make deeper meaning—a sense that matters—when we do so in the company of God. In the company of God the dots that matter and the connections made are more likely to enable the new we create for others to be meaningful, substantive and valuable. In the company of God we have both the criteria for selecting the dots that matter and the guidance to shape the character of their connections. In the company of God, both dots and their connections are "rooted and grounded in love."[6] Put cryptically, in the company of God plumb lines[7] will precede top lines and bottom lines, which benefits everyone.

What then makes for meaning? What is meaningful and how do we discern the more from the less meaningful, not just in the privacy of our own minds and hearts, but in public arenas as well?

MEANING

In understanding what makes for meaning, the hard physical sciences may have less to contribute than do the softer sciences of philosophy and theology. As Gordon Allport expressed it: "He who has a why to live can bear with almost any how."[8]

Allport's inspiration came from Victor Frankl who survived what would have been unbearable for most of us. As a prisoner of the Nazi concentration camp at Auschwitz, Frankl found himself "stripped to naked existence," losing his father, mother, brother and wife to the same concentration camp system in which he found himself. But even in these circumstances Frankl found meaning in his devotion to something (or some one) greater than himself.

---

6. Eph 3:17.
7. Amos 7:7–8.
8. Frankl, *Man's Search for Meaning*, 12.

First published in 1946, the book's popularity sent it through multiple printings. In Frankl's own preface to the 1983 edition, he looks back on the book's success and offers readers this suggestion:[9]

> Don't aim at success—the more you aim at it and make it a target, the more you are going to miss it. For success, like happiness, cannot be pursued; it must ensue, and it only does so as the unintended side-effect of one's personal dedication to a cause greater than oneself or as the by-product of one's surrender to a person other than oneself.

A cause greater is at least one of the dots that must be connected to other dots if meaning is to be made. Such a dot is teleological if not theological. It is a "super dot" that ties together threads of meaning, purpose and value implicit in other dots and connections.

If we are going to make meaning before money[10] then sooner or later we need to understand value. Value is variously understood but it is always derivative of purpose.

Change stimulates sense-making in both individuals and organizations. And when we find ourselves trying to make sense of change, not only for ourselves but also for others and indeed *with* others, we are unlikely to get very far without an adequate understanding of what we often assume we understand—*value*.

VALUE

The word derives from the French word *valoir*, from the Latin *valere*, meaning "be strong" or "be worth." In English, connotations vary depending on whether the word form is a singular noun, a plural noun, or a verb.

As a singular noun (value), equivalence is the connotation first noted in the dictionary: "that amount of a commodity, or medium of exchange, considered to be an equivalent for something else or a fair or satisfactory equivalent or return."[11] For example, when we say "that's good value for the money" we deemed it worth the cost incurred, whether in money, time, attention or devotion. Equivalence, however, is chronically vulnerable to

---

9. Ibid., 16.

10. Money is often confused with value, though it is really a means of exchange, a medium of storage (for exchange value), and a standard of equivalence.

11. *New Shorter Oxford Annotated Dictionary*, s.v. "value."

equivocation, particularly if there is no common standard or criteria by which equivalence is determined.

As a plural noun (values) the connotation shifts to moral matters. Even such a slight change—the simple addition of an "s"—illustrates how ready we are to divorce the moral from the economic. Such a divorce may comfort us with a convenient compartmentalization, but it leaves us lounging on the couch of moral relativism. What is right and fitting for one context may not be for another.

As a verb ("to value" something or someone), the act of appraisal is front and center. Without some common standard, however, every appraisal remains an estimate at best and equivocation at worst. When we value something or someone we cannot escape *evaluating*. As evaluators we put ourselves in the judgment seat. Is this person, place or thing worth the expense of our money, time, attention, or devotion? When we value someone (even ourselves) or something, we typically endow the person, place or thing with a worth that is greater than another. Comparative logic is difficult to avoid. *Discrimination* is unavoidable.[12]

Upon what basis do we evaluate? Theology has much to say about this basis. Economics tends to avoid the question, if it can. Ethics is hard-pressed to avoid relativism. Many will insist that a category error is being made when economics and ethics intersect. Some would prefer that economic value remain unrelated to ethical value and vice versa.

This separation, however, may not hold up when closely scrutinized. Simply from a theological point of view, to imagine that God's interests are confined to moral not economic matters is in effect putting limits on God's interests. To suggest that God is not interested in how evaluations are conducted is clearly as untenable as is the absolutist position that God judges everything and everyone harshly.

VALUE LAYERS

Topsoil, subsoil and bedrock present a useful way to think about value. Common expressions like "deeper meaning" or the "real value hidden underneath," suggest that, like soil, value is layered as well. Like layers of soil, the layers of value lack sharp, well-defined boundaries between them, and no one layer alone is sufficient for life and growth. All are necessary

---

12. In contrast is the repeated biblical imperative to "show no partiality" found in Luke 20:21; 1 Tim 5:21; Acts 10:24; and Jas 2:1–13.

and work together. In fact, meaning and value come from the integration among and between the layers. Even bedrock influences subsoil. Soil scientists refer to the influence of the bedrock as "parent material."

What grows is nourished by soil that holds its roots. What is growing and how fast is more visible at the layer of topsoil, for sure. But what is more difficult to see is what goes on just under the surface, where nutrients make themselves available to seeds germinating before breaking through the surface.

This is the case for value as viewed by individuals, organizations, communities or whole societies. Markets are the top layer of value. Markets are typically where value is seen and recognized. The origins of value, however, germinate from the subsoil and bedrock underneath. When it comes to understanding the structure of value, no one layer alone is sufficient, for growth or life.

Following this analogy, value can be described as having three basic layers: the transactional (topsoil), the instrumental (the subsoil in the middle) and the intrinsic (the underlying bedrock). Each deserves consideration.

"Exchange" or "market" value are terms economists use to refer to the topsoil of *transactional value*. Equivalency is their primary concern, based on quantitative and monetary standards agnostic to context. Examples include the exchange of an employee's experience for pay in an employment agreement, or a box of cereal on the grocery shelf exchanged for cash at the checkout counter. Equivalency lasts only for relatively short periods of time, given various other forces affecting fluctuations of transactional value.

The subsoil of *instrumental value* is interested in the function or purpose of the product, system or program. "Means value" or "value-in-use" are other designations for instrumental value. Estimating the value at this layer is context dependent. The particular context in which the thing is used or the person is employed determines its value. For example, the value of a pizza cutter in and of itself is not much, except when it is used to cut a freshly baked pizza. Its value is realized as and when it is used, less the costs associated with storing it, cleaning it and even using it. The use context determines the value at this layer. This middle layer value is often assessed in terms of *practice* or application. At this layer, value is calibrated in terms of measurable *performance*. In fact this layer could also be called the performance layer where value and performance is more easily seen, measured and compared.

The bedrock of *intrinsic value* represents what is important regardless of use, context or equivalency. Intrinsic value is typically considered a moral or ethical standard or virtue, like trustworthiness, justice, love, kindness, and honesty. "Intrinsic" suggests that the value comes from within. It is inherent to the thing or person, regardless of external conditions. Intrinsic value is qualitative more than quantitative and persists across varying contexts and conditions. Likewise at this layer, value is often defined as a *principle*—what is true and valid regardless of the contextual differences.

These three layers of value are often viewed as separate—even mutually exclusive—and often applied differently, depending upon whether people or objects are the focus of attention. Classical economics separates transactional and instrumental value from intrinsic value. Economics justifies this by claiming that economics is primarily interested in the transactional or instrumental values of goods rather than people. Classical economics typically absolves itself of concerns regarding intrinsic value, leaving these concerns to ethics. This effectively excludes ethical considerations from economic analysis, all because intrinsic values are regarded as something different and disassociated from extrinsic ones. This disassociation leads to a persistent "de-lamination" of value.

The persistence of this de-lamination may reflect the absence of a theological perspective. Bring theological perspective to these layers and fresh questions arise. Might the widening gap between the accumulating wealth of the one percent and the declining wealth of the rest be symptomatic of this de-lamination, particularly when the financial economy becomes increasingly disassociated from the real economy? Can substantive value or meaning be created in a transactional layer alone? Mustn't such meaning also penetrate into and through the instrumental layer and to intrinsic value as well, if it is to matter?

De-lamination may be cognitively convenient by keeping things categorically neat and tidy. In reality, however, the three are inseparable. For example, commercial organizations concern themselves with both transactional and instrumental value and yet must comply within the constraints of intrinsic values. If they ignore intrinsic value, they risk erosion of societal and customer trust. Without this connection to intrinsic value the company can be out of business in very short order. Remember the world's largest accounting firm, Arthur Anderson? When it lost the trust of society and clients it vanished in less than a year.

This de-lamination may also infect nonprofit organizations that we imagine are more concerned with intrinsic value. However, to the extent that these organizations ignore the subsoil and topsoil of instrumental and transactional value—measurable impact, outcome and effectiveness—these organizations risk losing contributions from current and future donors, not to mention the trust of the communities they serve.

Who is to say that what we are engaged in can't carry intrinsic, instrumental and transactional value at the same time? The more meaning we make, the more value layers this meaning will penetrate and intersect. Isn't this typically what we mean when we admiringly attribute something with a deeper value—a value that money can't buy? This is what we are invited to do when in the company of God.

If we are to make meaning before money, if we are to make sense of change and create new value for others, surely one or more of the dots that we connect will need to be found in the subsoil of instrumental value if not the bedrock of intrinsic value. The "good soil" Jesus referred to in his parable of the sower[13] is likely a soil of all three layers.

When all the dots we find to connect originate from the topsoil of transactional value alone—represented by quantitative data or so-called "big data"—the value we create and the meaning we make will be thin at best and likely short lived.[14] This echoes Jesus' own interpretation of the parable of the sower.[15] The soil of the hard path invited the tweeting birds to come along and eat them up. The soil of the rocky ground had insufficient depth. Scorching sun withered the little sprouts quickly. The seeds that fell among thorns were choked by "the cares of the world and the lure of wealth" such that they yielded nothing. It is only in the good soil of instrumental and intrinsic value that seeds can bear fruit and yield, "in one case a hundredfold, in another sixty, and in another thirty." Apparently it matters in what kind of soil the dots (seeds) take root.

With this layered view of value in mind we can look more closely at how meaning can be made and value can be created.

13. Matt 13:3–34; Mark 4:3–32; Luke 8:5–15.

14. Meadows, *Thinking in Systems*, 194. Meadows made the observation that numbers are the least effective basis upon which to intervene in a system, from which could be inferred that numbers are the least effective "dots" to start with in making meaning in response to change.

15. Matt 13:4–7, 22–23.

WHICH DOTS TO CONNECT

"Connect the dots" is an apt expression for making sense of change. It also describes something most of us can do.

That most of us can do this turns out to be a very good thing, given how necessary it is for making sense. However, our increasingly connected era seems to be giving us too many dots to connect and ways to connect them. "We're going to find ourselves in the not too distant future swimming in sensors and drowning in data," observed Lt. Gen. David Deptula in 2010.[16] The sea of sensors and the flood of data are slated to rise even more with the emerging "Internet of Things." Will this be another flood of biblical proportions—this time a flood of data?

Making meaning and money depends as much upon the dots we select as it does on the character and quality of the connections we make. Selecting may be what we still have to learn. As dots and ways to connect them proliferate, the dots we choose and how we connect them will become only more important. Our cultural atmosphere is already drenched with data and saturated with unseen signals crisscrossing the atmosphere and incessantly skipping between cell towers. With all this connectedness, some are asking whether we are really communicating anything or not, and if we are, is the content of our communications meaningful. Is all this connective capacity and capability leading us to more, better or deeper meaning and value?

MIT's Sherry Turkle believes not. Turkle observes that all this connectivity is causing us to expect more from technology and less from each other. Citing analysis of data from over fourteen thousand college students over the past thirty years Turkle suggests we are "connected as we've never been connected before, and we seem to have damaged ourselves in the process."[17] She points to the disturbing findings from a University of Michigan's Institute for Social Research study:

> Since the year 2000, young people have reported a dramatic decline in interest in other people. Today's college students are, for example, far less likely to say that it is valuable to try to put oneself in the place of others or to try to understand their feelings. The authors of this study associate students' lack of empathy with the availability of online games and social network. An online connection can be deeply felt, but you only need to deal with the part of the person you see in your game world or social network. . . . One

16. Magnuson, "Military 'Swimming in Sensors.'"
17. Turkle, *Alone Together*, 293.

might say that absorbed in those they have "friended," children lose interest in friendship. . . . Their detachment is not aggressive. It is as though they just don't see the point.[18]

Making sense of change is not about more and faster data. It is about making meaning. It is about trusting our abilities to perceive, decipher what dots to connect and creatively connect them in coherent and compassionate ways. This is what it takes to make sense, meaning and ultimately new value for others in response to change. Technology can help us make the connections, at least initially. But something besides technology will be necessary to make sense, meaning and value from the connections. In the company of God, this something just may be theology more than technology.

CONNECTING DOTS

Connecting the dots is not just a familiar expression. It's a familiar experience. But to understand how meaning is made and value is created in the act of connecting dots we need to get behind the colloquial expression. How does connecting the dots create the content and form of meaning and value?

Karl Weick, and others, explain it this way: meaning requires three things—a past "frame," a present "cue," and an association between them.

> The lack of prototypical past moments . . . can prolong the search for meaning. Frames tend to be past moments of socialization and cues tend to be present moments of experience. If a person can construct a relationship between these two moments, meaning is created. This means that the content of sense-making is to be found in the frames and categories that summarize past experience, in the cues and labels that snare specifics of present experience, and in the ways these two settings of experience are connected.[19]

A past frame, a present cue, and an association between the two, form a "minimal sensible structure" which is what we create when we make sense of change. It also shows up in creating new value for others. Minimal sensible structures may come in enmeshed multiples as well; like Edwin Friedman's "interlocking emotional triangles,"[20] these minimal sensible structures comprise the fabric of the meaning we make to navigate life,

18. Ibid.
19. Weick, *Sensemaking in Organizations*, 111.
20. Friedman, *Failure of Nerve*, 204.

private and personal as well as public and societal. All this is but a more technical way of describing what most of us are quite familiar with already.

Not all dots, of course, are equal. Neither are all connections. The minimal sensible structures connect different dots in different ways. The meaning that can be made and the new value that can be created from connecting the dots is a function not only of the number and nature of the dots we connect. It is also a function of the strength of the connections themselves. When we bring a theological perspective to the dots, frames and the connections, the minimal sensible structures we create take on a deeper meaning. With a theological lens the dots we pay attention to, the connections we draw and the frames we use will more likely seek transformational rather than transactional value.

Remember the workbooks in early elementary school instructing us to connect the dots? Who among us hasn't had an experience of penciling lines between sequentially numbered dots on a page? Drawing lines between numbered dots gives us the simple pleasure of watching a form emerge. When the form begins to emerge we experience the pleasure of a modest "aha" experience. A piece of the puzzle falls into place. Dots connect. Meaning is made, or perhaps more accurately, discovered. What we couldn't quite see before, now we can see more clearly, at least in part.

Three decades of facilitating creative problem-solving and invention sessions have left me with the conviction that everyone has the ability to connect the dots. It is an individual competence, enhanced by collaborating with others, to be sure. But as an individual skill it is innate in us all, regardless of how well or poorly we may assess our own connection-making competence.

When making sense of substantive change we naturally look for a "deeper meaning." The phrase suggests that meaning resides under the surface. It presumes that what we see and experience on the surface is only a part of the story. We assume the real or underlying meaning—the sense we make of change—comes from a root cause under the surface. The same can be said for value. Meaning is never far from what people regard as the *underlying value.*

Certainly there are different attitudes toward this habit of looking for the deeper meaning and underlying value. Many of us are content to remain close to the surface finding sufficient meaning there. Others of us have a longing to go deeper. Even among those who long for deeper meaning there are different degrees of depth that prove satisfying. Some won't stop digging for a deeper meaning until they hit the bedrock of intrinsic value or even the hot molten core below it. For others it may be entirely sufficient to stop digging when they discover something practical that works for their immediate need.

Regardless of our own propensities and patience, the connections we make will need to find dots at deeper layers than at the layer of topsoil alone. If we make sense only at the transactional layer of value we may make money but it will be without much meaning.

MONEY WITHOUT MEANING

No one literally "makes money" of course, except for the central banks or national treasuries, at least as and when nations choose to increase their country's money supply. Businesses and individuals do not "make" money unless they are counterfeiting. It is interesting, though, how often we use this expression even as a synonym for "making a living." Suffice it to say, money is deeply entangled in our patterns of thought, speech and behavior, so much so that it may be impossible to see it for what it actually is.

Money itself is unique among other commodities. It is a means of exchange, a common standard for comparing values and a means of storing value which when stored can generate more money through interest. Because of these attributes—especially the combination of these attributes—money easily becomes not only de-laminated from the other layers of value. It can become its own layer of value. As and when it disengages from the instrumental or intrinsic layers of value, money becomes its own power and principality and a very powerful one at that (though not particularly principled).

When our intent is to make money regardless of the sense, meaning or value, a longing remains unsatisfied, even when plenty of money is "made." This unsatisfied longing is a sign and symptom of the absence of meaning at the transactional and instrumental layers. A sense of meaning and purpose greater than ourselves is missing, as may be the incarnation of this value at the instrumental layer.

Transactional value alone can be like empty calories. There is energy there to be sure, energy that can be derived, converted and stored. However, there is little nutrition and by itself, it represents an unsustainable, unhealthy diet.

As it turns out, there are many ways to make money other than making sense, meaning or new value for others. These other ways may be increasing in number and even in their respective ability to make money without meaning: selling short, trading in derivatives, collecting interest and all other forms of speculation, to name a few.

Idolatry is theology's term for making money without meaning. It is a particularly prevalent, persistent and ancient form of idolatry. From a secular viewpoint idolatry would not even come to mind. It doesn't even show up unless we include a theological frame in our sense-making.

The interest theology has here is as much practical as it is doctrinal, especially in the context of sense-making and value creation. Avoiding illusions and delusions that plague sense-making and innovating is essential. Idolatry is illusion and delusion, and theology's concern with idolatry can be quite practical. There are at least two reasons for this.

The first is that technically idolatry is showing devotion and ascribing meaning to some thing (or some one) that doesn't deserve it. Practically, idolatry is accompanied by emotional obsession and cognitive compulsion. Both misdirect time, attention and devotion, not unlike the emotional obsessions that accompany physical addiction.

The desire for more is at the heart of this idolatry. Jesus gave it the name *mammon*—a quirky Aramaic expression—which is often translated "wealth." Wealth suggests accumulation. Jesus made it clear that in his opinion mammon is always in direct competition with God for our time, attention and devotion. Mammon vies with God to be our master. Neither can be truly a master if we try to serve both simultaneously.[21]

Accumulation, and especially accumulation far beyond what one needs, is the illusory power animating and enabling money to become the idol that it can so easily become.

The actual idolatry here, however, is the time, attention and devotion in the pursuit of "more." In the parable of the dishonest manager[22] this form of idolatry is linked to capacity, even more than the nature of the content filling that capacity. It's about having more than is necessary. Or as Matthew puts it, storing up treasure where moth and rust consume and thieves break in and steal.[23]

While mammon may be the idolatry, money is the idol. As an idol it can take on various forms: coin, paper or electrons. But as an idol it has no reality beyond what it represents—a means, medium and standard. Money

---

21. Matt 6:24; Luke 16:9, 11, 13.

22. Luke 16:1–13.

23. Matt 6:19–20.

by itself is not the root of evil.[24] Idols are by definition man-made, empty. Their reality is illusion. Idols have little if any intrinsic value, except perhaps for the gold from which they are made. The meaning they hold is totally imputed to them, endowed by the misdirected longings of those who give the idol their time, attention and devotion. While idol*atry* is the undue devotion to accumulation—wanting more than we really need—money is the *idol*, one with a potency that may be increasing.

In his book *Theology of Money* Philip Goodchild observes that in the modern world the limitations of money have been overcome by the perception of money as valuable in and of itself. No longer is money seen as simply a means of exchange, medium of storage and standard by which to compare values. Money has taken on its own power, a power that competes with the power of God. Goodchild puts it this way:

> Where God promises eternity, money promises the world. Where God offers a delayed reward, money offers a reward in advance. Where God offers himself as grace, money offers itself as a loan. Where God offers spiritual benefits, money offers tangible benefits. Where God accepts all repentant sinners who truly believe, money may be accepted by all who are willing to trust in its value. Where God requires conversion of the soul, money empowers the existing desires and plans of the soul. Money has the advantages of immediacy, universality, tangibility, and utility. Money promises freedom and gives a down payment on the promise of prosperity.[25]

Money is a potent, prevalent and persistent idol. As an idol money may have become more powerful than other idols in its rivalry with God.

The second reason to invoke the notion of idolatry is to differentiate money and its accumulation from the positive intent of God. In doing so, we must clarify just what that positive intent is.

If God truly has our best interests at heart, then the prohibition against idolatry is as much a function of God's concern for what is good and healthy for us as it is a function of divine jealousy. Making money without meaning—without instrumental or intrinsic value, or both—is not healthy for us, whether we are thinking of the health of individuals, organizations or society as a whole. When meaning is confined to the transactional layer, what takes precedence is what we can "get out of" life, experiences or relationships. It remains a thin topsoil sure to dry up and erode before too long.

24. 1 Tim 6:10—"the *love* of money is the root of all kinds of evil."
25. Goodchild, *Theology of Money*, 11.

The idolatry of accumulation has a close association with the transactional layer. This layer is comprised of outcomes and outputs. It is the easiest to measure and count. But just because it can be counted—whatever it is—doesn't necessarily mean it counts. "The paradox of accounting is that it directs attention to what is counted rather than to what matters."[26] What matters is that which demands our time, attention and devotion, which the human sciences of wealth ignore. The science of wealth only studies the outcomes of economic activity. "The investigation of the powers and principles by which time, attention and devotion are distributed should belong, by contrast, to the discipline of theology."[27]

Devotion to accumulation is measured quantitatively often to the exclusion of qualitative considerations. This leads to all sorts of distortions in what is regarded as meaningful and valuable. Transactional value trumps intrinsic value or becomes so divorced from any recognizable connection with intrinsic value that we lose our grounding in what really matters. The sense made in these more surface contexts may indeed create monetary wealth, but it is hollow not hallowed. It may exist in some fashion, but it remains without meaning. It provides security without substance, solutions without sustainability.

Many individuals and organizations with established revenue streams often become obsessed with the metrics of what is valuable. They are governed by a transactional mind-set (e.g., accounting, metrics, quantifications). They often look to markets and transactions for ways to accumulate or save rather than commit and create. But it is in spending—especially time, attention and devotion—and from intrinsic value that new value is created and meaning is made.

Making meaning is much easier when we know what makes for meaning to begin with. When we already have a sense for what is meaningful and what is not, then we are already part of the way there. Not knowing what makes for meaning is equivocation. Here is where theology offers tremendous practical advantage over purely secular perspectives. In the company of God, plumb lines precede top lines or bottom lines. A primary goal of theology is to keep the plumb lines front and center.

26. Ibid., 24.
27. Ibid., 7.

MEANING WITHOUT VALUE

Making meaning without value may be less pervasive. But it is just as debilitating a misdirection of attention and effort. If the dots that resonate with intrinsic principles do not link with dots in some context of practice, any meaning that might be made will likely remain as empty and lifeless as an idol.

Principle must find its form in practice. The language of invention calls this "preferred embodiment" or "the reduction to practice." The language of theology calls this incarnation or the "scandal of particularity." But whether we are using the idioms of invention or theology, the type of connection is the same. It is a connection that crosses the boundary between theory and practice, between the ideal and the real, between intrinsic value in the context-less realm of principle and the instrumental value of a specific context and practice.

Meaning without value may be produced in a consumer economy more often than we care to admit. How much is difficult to say. In part, the amount may be manifest in what percent of the overall economy is engaged in activities related to advertising and promotion. What the Philadelphia retailer John Wannamaker said years ago still seems to hold true: "Half the money I spend on advertising is wasted and the trouble is that I don't know which half."

But whether in marketing, producing or innovating, value is not the neat and tidy concept accountants might like us to believe it is. Nor at the other end of the continuum is value resident in the pristine ideal ethicists might secretly want us to think it is. What or who is important and valuable to one person may not be to another. Neither economics nor ethics can completely escape erosions into relativism and even subjectivism.

A recent attempt to escape this relativism is Robert and Edward Skidelsky's book *How Much Is Enough: Money and the Good Life* (2012). From an economic and philosophical perspective the Skidelskys propose a rough set of universal and indispensable intrinsic values.[28] There are seven: health, security, respect, personality,[29] harmony with nature, friendship and leisure. Living a life that realizes all of these is what it means to live the good life, at least in the view of this economist and his philosopher/ethicist son. To be fair, the Skidelskys recognize the difficulty in realizing these intrinsic,

---

28. Skidelsky and Skidelsky, *How Much Is Enough*, 150–67.

29. Ibid., 160–61. Here the Skidelskys suggest independence sufficient for choice-making.

principled and "pure" values in the real world. But what seems to interest the Skidelskys are the potential conflicts between these values, rather than the embodiments of these values themselves.

Theology has an essential contribution to make here. Theology is much more familiar with the paradox at the center of the idea that God "scandalously" shows up in local and particular circumstances and that when God is involved (when is God not?) both the specific and the universal are also. Philip Goodchild expresses it this way:

> Theology, concerned with the ultimate criteria of life, is the most fundamental and radical inquiry. It attempts to discern how truth, goodness, and life come to be constituted. It offers to the world a vision of life interpreted according to the richest categories of meaning. It has the duty to invest life with the deepest layers of spiritual wealth—that is, it has to determine what is the nature of true wealth. This is the vocation for theology, whether Christian or not, and it is the most fundamental inquiry, whether pursued by believers, nonbelievers, or no one at all. Worldly wealth, which can only mean exchange value in terms of money, is to be judged against a new revelation of divine power.[30]

Goodchild goes on to suggest that theology is uniquely positioned for the task of evaluating all values,[31] which is nothing less that what Jesus saw himself doing. His central message is "repent, for the kingdom of heaven is at hand," essentially a reevaluation of what and how we value what is meaningful.

Businesses and organizations often relegate ethical issues to matters of compliance. Theology, on the other hand, if it steps up to its vocation, will strike at the root of both an organization's purpose and strategy, the way it operates to produces value and the value it produces. Theology asks whether this value is worth producing, not because money is to be made, but because meaning, sense and intrinsic value for people's lives are at stake.

The last parable Jesus tells in Luke's Gospel is a direct challenge to the propensity of making meaning without value.[32] In this parable a leader goes out of town on an extended trip. Before leaving he calls together his direct reports and gives each varying amounts of money with which to trade during his absence. Upon his return he asks, quite naturally, how each performed with what each had been entrusted. The ones to whom he had entrusted

---

30. Godchild, *Theology of Money*, 4.

31. Ibid., 5.

32. Luke 19:1–27.

more came back with returns of ten and five times earnings, performances that garnered each of them even more favor, trust and responsibility. In contrast was the one who returned only what he had *preserved*. He had "given back" only what the leader had given him, largely out of a conserving fear and narrow ignorance of the leader's own intention and commitment. Jesus concludes the parable with a rather harsh "I tell you, to all those who have, more will be given; but from those who have nothing, even what they have will be taken away." Such is the fate of the organization that remains in its own comfort zone of preservation rather than innovation.

The last one placed what he received under the mattress. He remained in the pristine and private layer of intrinsic value, principled but essentially afraid. He kept it to himself and unlike the others, took no risk in deploying what he had been given. The result was valueless meaning, lifeless existence and even further loss of what little he had been given.

Socrates famously claimed the unexamined life is not worth living. To this Socratic truth might be added the unengaged life is not worth examining. A purpose greater than ourselves cannot remain in some abstract, undeployed state of isolation, preserved and conserved. Even a principled dot with meaning and purpose will die the death of irrelevance without being connected to a particular place, person or thing in a specific context—in other words, without committing to practice.

All this reflects John Gardner's observation that "the society which scorns excellence in plumbing as a humble activity and tolerates shoddiness in philosophy because it is an exalted one will have neither good plumbing nor good philosophy; neither its pipes nor its theories will hold water."[33] With no pipe between layers of intrinsic and instrumental value, genuine meaning, sense and value are difficult to discern and make. Making sense that means something to another ushers us directly into the instrumental value layer—the middle layer—where all value and meaning is shaped by the local context.

MAKING IT IN THE MIDDLE LAYER

If the meaning we make matters to others—ourselves and even with God—then the making of it will command our time, attention and devotion. It will require us to show up, pay attention and give ourselves to the particularity

---

33. Gardner was the Secretary of Health, Education and Welfare in the Johnson administration.

of the local circumstances of a specific context, including its people, place and circumstances.

Such commitments do not come easily to individuals and organizations defining themselves only by the transactional topsoil. The specific and local is uninteresting to those invested in scale or leverage. These are concerns native to the quantitative. In fact, when we are at the layer of topsoil, meaning has already been made. At this layer meaning and value is now being distributed, extended or extracted. The *making* of meaning however, occurs at the middle layer—the layer of practice—where concerns are qualitative and relational more than quantitative and transactional. Isn't this what Jesus points to in his attention to the one lost sheep, not being satisfied with the ninety-nine who are not lost?[34] Clearly there is a view of value here beyond the numbers.

In the context of commercial organizations, profits are the signs and symptoms that new value for others *has been* made. The making of it happens at a different level altogether. This distinction caused Clayton Christensen to counsel innovators in their attempts to make meaning to be patient for growth and impatient for profits. Profit is a more reliable indicator of new value for others than growth in the commercial sphere.

If what Christensen suggests is true, then entrepreneurial success stories based on exponential growth, like Facebook and Twitter and others, might give us pause to carefully examine whether their meaning and value links to anything deeper in the intrinsic layer of value. The slogan "think globally, act locally" might be amended with "start locally." Similarly, for a nonprofit organization its outcomes and impacts are signs that meaning has been made, but the making of it happens at the instrumental layer.

The intent here is not to disparage outcome or its limited orientation to value. There is nothing inherently wrong with scalable initiatives, just as there is nothing inherently more righteous or redemptive about them. The intent rather is to suggest that meaning and substantive value is more likely to be made at the middle layer and that this middle layer is first and foremost governed by local context. This is the "scandal of particularity." The more classical theological principle is incarnation.

The principle of incarnation for theology, embodiment for patenting and particularity for the globally minded, is as much paradox as it is scandalous. Paradox is always problematic for those inclined to logic, rationality or reason. The biblical witness is scandalous however, in its narrative and poetic

---

34. Luke 15:1–7.

retelling of Israel's tumultuous and far-from-stable relationship with God. It bears witness to a God who is not confined to human logic, reason or even some Aristotelian or Platonic standard of rationality. God is free to do as and when God pleases. Otherwise God would not be God. If it is God's choice to commit to a specific time and place, to a specific people, even display what might otherwise be considered to be a discriminatory (though perhaps purposeful) choice of some rather than others, while simultaneously loving and committing to all, then who are we to suggest otherwise?

Of course, we do suggest otherwise, and often. As and when we do, we reveal only our own presumptions and bias for neat and tidy logic more than revealing anything about God. This divine reality—an embarrassingly persistent contradiction to our penchant for thinking *we* are God's agents and understand God—is what Walter Brueggemann calls the "agency of *God*."[35]

The idea of divine agency is also a scandal, at least to the educated, sophisticated and enlightened. It is the idea that God not only exists, but is willing, able and active in intervening in particular and local affairs, not according to our standards of coherence and logic and presumptions about phenomenology, but from God's standards of faithfulness, righteousness, loving kindness and mercy. God seems to choose to act and invites us to act in particular contexts, each with its own purpose. This is the franchise, territory or domain, if you will, of the company of God, the reign of God on earth.

This middle, instrumental layer is where meaning is made and new value is created for others. This has not completely escaped the awareness of worldly companies sensitive to the vulnerabilities of trying to survive in an information and knowledge economy. In the book *The Knowledge Creating Company*, Ikujiro Nonaka and Hirotaka Takeuchi proposed that it is not what a company knows that creates wealth.[36] Rather, it is the company's ability to *create new knowledge that matters*—i.e., knowledge that carries instrumental value. This ability turns out to be the real source of wealth creation, not simply knowing something. As a result, much of Nonaka and Takeuchi's attention is given over to how knowledge that has value is created.

They describe a set of four different processes all of which share conversion, interestingly enough, as the essential process. All four of these conversion processes represent instances of dot-connecting and dot-converting.

---

35. Walter Brueggemann's comments made at the Fuller Forum (spring 2015) "Justice, Grace and Law in the Mission of God."

36. Nonaka and Takeuchi, *Knowledge-Creating Company*, 3–7, 56–94.

The four conversions are socialization, externalization, combination and internalization.

Socialization consists of tacit-to-tacit conversions of knowledge. For example, when two practitioners get together and talk shop and one or both of them get an idea they go and use. *Externalization* consists of tacit-to-explicit conversions of knowledge. For example when an expert commits his or her know-how into an explicit expression in writing, a presentation or some codified form. In the process of expressing this knowledge there is often new knowledge created. I have witnessed this new knowledge creation repeatedly as inventors come to a new awareness of their own invention when they work with a patent attorney who puts it on paper in drafting a patent application. *Combination* consists of explicit-to-explicit conversions of codified or published knowledge. For example when one discipline's codified knowledge links up with another's codified knowledge in another field as in the case of interdisciplinary studies. *Internalization* consists of the explicit-to-tacit conversions of codified knowledge into an act or routine of a practitioner in action.

New value also comes from these conversions of understanding, in context and on purpose. Seeing and recognizing new value is more about redrawing contextual boundaries and reframing content, less about calculating outcomes with precise metrics. The one who sees value where others do not is the one French economist J. B. Say first named an entrepreneur. The entrepreneur is one who takes a low value material—a material that others reject because of its commonness—and brings it into a higher value use.[37] The entrepreneur doesn't change the properties of the material. Rather, the entrepreneur sees in the material a contribution it can make to a specific context and purpose. Context sculpts value. There is no value without context.

What looks like a reversal of the relative value of a material, from worthless waste to a key ingredient, is not a transformation of the material by any supernatural or transubstantial magic. Rather, it is the introduction of a context to the material, or perhaps the reverse, the introduction of the material to a context.

Many successful companies make the mistake of looking for large opportunities, believing that by analysis they will be able to spot such large-scale opportunities. They ignore the reality that what becomes large first starts small, even at first, rejected. "The stone which the builders rejected

37. Drucker, *Innovation and Entrepreneurship*, 21.

has become the head of the corner. This is the Lord's doing and it is marvelous in our eyes."[38]

The rejected stone of Psalm 118, quoted not only in the gospels of Matthew, Mark and Luke[39], was also cited by Peter,[40] the rock upon which Jesus said he would build his church, the "get-behind-me-Satan" rock whom Jesus rejected, the rock that denied Jesus three times, and the one who apparently had his own challenges with emotional self-regulation.

Does the gospel really mean to say that it has a bias for inferior quality materials and broken rocks? Does it really mean to say that the kingdom of God is constructed and built not only with low value material but even with material that has been rejected, discarded, considered waste? Is the gospel some kind of spiritual recovery, reuse, and recycling principal?

All of this should give us a big pause regarding what (and who) we regard as valuable, how we assign value and the ways we measure it. The value scheme of the world resides on a different base than the value scheme of the gospel.

Both references of Jesus to the rejected stone come in narrative contexts in which scribes and Pharisees question his authority. The scribes and Pharisees want Jesus to claim his authority. But instead, Jesus asks them a question regarding *their* authority, promising to reciprocate an answer to their question once they answer his.

Why the cat and mouse game here around the question of authority? I sense that Jesus knew that real authority is not claimed. It is recognized. Similarly, real value is not claimed or assigned. It is recognized. This is not only a spiritual truth. It is an entrepreneurial reality. When value is assigned from the top down rather than recognized from the bottom up, the value is transactional and performance oriented. It tends to be imposed.

This does not imply that the desire to perform is an unworthy goal. However, the motivation to improve our performance is less likely to create new value for others. It may improve the numbers and relative value may increase. But when we start from the transaction layer it tends toward repetition and imitation rather than innovation and the creation of new value. If we are looking for substantive dots to connect and we look for them in the numbers, we will always be looking in retrospect. Retrospect might promise us the benefits of hindsight, including a level of precision.

38. Ps 118:22–23.
39. Matt 21:42; Mark 12:10; Luke 20:17.
40. Acts 4:11 and 1 Pet 2:4–7, citing Isa 28:16.

But it will always be the "hinds" we are sighting. Making sense of change that leads to creating new value for others necessitates foresight.

STARTING BELOW BEDROCK

This brings us to the question of where to start. Where do we begin the search for dots to connect? If it is not from the transactional level, then should we start with dots that are instrumental or intrinsic? Or should we be starting from some other place?

If we enter the instrumental value layer from a starting point of intrinsic value we are more likely to make meaning and create new value for others that matters. When principle motivates and animates practice, from the bottom-up so to speak, we are more likely to make deeper meaning and create new value that is more substantive. Peter Drucker named the most reliable places to start as "the unexpected" and "incongruities."[41] Theology might use different words, like "wonder" and "injustice," respectively. Regardless of the words used, they point to the same places to start. Bedrock.

Starting the search for dots in the bedrock is no mean feat in a pluralistic, multi-cultural world, even with a theological perspective. Once we start looking for dots at the intrinsic layer of value the search can quickly turn into a wandering in the wilderness of equivocation. Competing mind-sets, ideologies and traditions, religious, cultural or otherwise, not to mention moral relativism, infect this bedrock of value and principle, particularly in a world that espouses different views on what these principles are, not to mention how these principles are understood.

Extend the soils analogy deeper still and we find a hot, molten core—as much energy as matter—under the layer of bedrock. Without a theological acknowledgement of this single core, the bedrock will remain a shifting foundation layer—tectonic plates of intrinsic value subject to different cultures, frames and points of view.

Underneath this bedrock, however, is a deeper single core that theology acknowledges as the source of all meaning and value. This single core, of course, is God. This single core may have been what Jesus spoke of as the sum of all the commandments and ordinances—to love God and neighbor as yourself.[42] All other values—intrinsic, instrumental and even transactional—are derivations or corruptions of this one core. This core is pure

41. Drucker, *Innovation and Entrepreneurship*, 35.
42. Lev 19:18; Matt 19:19; 22:39; Mark 12:31–34; Luke 10:27; Rom 13:9; Jas 2:8.

generative energy emanating outward, generous, creative and creating. The molten core under the bedrock is the hot love of God.

As it emanates and extends outward with centrifugal expansion it will encounter crusted expressions of bedrock, often viewed as fixed, propositional and permanent. From the point of view of the core, however, the bedrock principles—commandments or short lists of intrinsic value—appear as hardened but brittle legacies where the hot energy of love has cooled and left a residual crust.

However, when we begin to look under the bedrock, we discover that value is more likely to come from what is "rooted and grounded" in love.[43] It emerges not from the transactional layer of value, but from what supports intrinsic and "living" value.

Making meaning before we attempt to make money will invite criticism from the skeptic. The skeptic imagines it naïve to think that if you build it they will come. Naïve though it may be, if you don't build it, they certainly will not come. The notion may be naïve but its alternative is despair, passivity or both.

The starting point for any creative act, whether on the part of the artist or the entrepreneur, is not money-making but meaning-making. This starting point will of necessity accept the very real risk that the meaning made may not make any money.[44]

> The artist who hopes to market work that is the realization of his gifts cannot begin with the market. He must create for himself that gift-sphere in which the work is made, and only when he knows that work to be the faithful realization of his gift should he turn to see if it has currency in that other economy. Sometimes it does, sometimes it doesn't.

The innovating organization that tries to make meaning and create new value for others cannot escape this risk either. But the organization that tries to avoid the risk at all costs, that seeks to save its own life, just may lose it.

43. Eph 3:17.
44. Hyde, *Gift*, 279.

7

The Company of God

THE LONE INNOVATOR OR sole entrepreneur is more fiction than fact. Heroes may dominate our innovation narratives but the realities of innovating take place in the company of others.

Look closely at the actual birth experience of companies. What we find are relationships. In the field of commercial innovations think Bill and Dave (Hewlett Packard), Walt and Roy (Disney), Gates and Allen (Microsoft), Jobs and Wozniak (Apple). In the field of social innovations think Millard and Linda Fuller and Clarence Jordon (Habitat for Humanity) or Bill W. and Dr. Bob (Alcoholics Anonymous). As much as we would like to believe the lone and heroic narrative of the individual entrepreneur, the reality is less about single parenting and more about high-trust relationships that broaden into the collectives we call companies. Companies do not guarantee success, of course. But entrepreneurial failure is likely without them.

Companies can hold our respect for their responsiveness. Others warrant our disdain for their bureaucracy. One might employ us, while for another we might wish to work. Some stretch across the globe while others remain local. Whatever their business and wherever they operate, companies seem as necessary and prevalent as they are useful.

"The company of God" is also a collective of individuals working toward a shared purpose. The expression and reality behind it, however, point to a greater purpose and different set of realities than those associated with the more visible companies of this world. As a surrogate expression for the kingdom of God on earth, "the company of God" is the subject of what follows. Both the expression itself and the realities behind it are worth considering as a central concept for innovation theology.

While often unseen, too often ignored and very different from companies of this world, the company of God "operates" in, through and among various worldly companies with which we are all familiar. The company of God may not choose to operate in every earthly company. But the notion that God might be interested and involved in these companies and their innovating efforts is neither unreasonable nor necessarily a new idea. And if there is any truth to this, then company leaders may want to consider how the innovating efforts of their companies align with the purpose and presence of the company of God.

The operations and innovations of the company of God do not depend upon our awareness. The company of God is there whether we see it or not. It has been quietly operating for quite some time. Likewise, it is prudent to remember that while the phrase "company of God" reminds us of God's presence, purpose and activity, it also implies the distinct possibility that others God chooses to involve in God's company—other individuals and companies—may not be ones we would choose. It's God's company after all, not ours.

As a way of describing God's involvement in change, the expression does not preempt divine interest in matters related to the salvation of an individual's soul. God's corporate interests do not obviate an interest in personal matters. God's interest and involvement in such company matters may actually envelope such individual concerns.

But first we should get a bit more comfortable with the expression itself and then take a closer look at the realities behind it before we consider the relevance for innovation theology.

THE EXPRESSION

As a surrogate for the kingdom of God on earth, "the company of God" may simply be easier on the ears. Kingdoms are unfamiliar to those fully enculturated to a democratic society. Democratic forms of government were not the political norm when Jesus used the phrase "kingdom of God." Neither were companies as much a part of the societal landscape then as they are now. Many, if not most of us, are simply more familiar with companies than kingdoms. Many of us have worked for one or more. A few of us have owned one, in whole or in part. Very few of us, however, have ever been subjects of a monarch, with interesting and obvious exceptions.

Currently our societal landscapes are saturated with companies. Their influence is considerable. Companies cross borders of many kinds, national, geographic and categorical. Not all of them are commercial organizations nor are all of them global. Many have other than economic purposes. Others root themselves deeply in local contexts. But whether global or local, economic or altruistic, every company will contend with change, sooner or later. And theologically speaking, sooner or later every company will either align with the company of God or not.

Not all companies are the same of course. Companies come in a wide variety of shapes and sizes, engage in a diverse spectrum of activities and represent a plethora of purposes. What *is* common among companies, however, is the association of individuals each working for a common or shared purpose. Common purpose is there, regardless of the separate and distinct agendas that each individual may have, such as a paycheck, contributions to a cause, or the gratification of deploying one's skills and expertise. What is common among kingdoms, however, is not so much the cause as the monarch.

The vocabulary of kingdoms—sovereignty, reign and realm—resonates with the imposition of order, the conservation of power and the location of authority. The vocabulary of companies on the other hand, resonates more closely with the adaptation and innovation required by change. "Company" may be unconventional, but it is not necessarily unorthodox or even heretical. It is not that "company" is more modern and "kingdom" is old fashioned. Rather, "company" may simply be more useful for the purposes of innovation theology. The freedom, activity and presence of God sound more applicable to innovation than sovereignty, reign and realm of God.

To be fair, "company" and "kingdom" have positive and negative associations earned from their long and varied histories. Neither maintains any immunity from nefarious examples of each. History is as replete with clueless kings and oppressive kingdoms as it is with corrupt companies and ventures that produce no value.

Unlike kingdoms, companies are defined and described in a variety of ways, including agency, ownership, capabilities, resources and interactions with the market and broader economy.[1] Relationships and transactions

---

1. Various points of view on the "theory of the firm" can be found on *Wikipedia*, one of the earliest of which at least in modern times was the transaction cost theory of Ronald Coase.

all play significant roles but differ according to perspective, interest and theory. For example, an accountant's perspective might describe a company as what is listed on its balance sheet: assets, liabilities, and the net equity left over. An investor might describe a company as a collection of tangible and intangible assets, with a current flow of operations (and cash) as well as a potential for growth. A systems thinker might describe a company as a dynamic system comprised of an evolving sequence of past, present and prospective interactions with its ecosystem of clients, customers, owners, suppliers, markets and competitors. A leader and manager might describe the company in terms of its organizational purpose, people, practices and what it produces. A legal perspective might define a company as a fictitious person with all the rights of a real person along with a legal limit to the personal liability of owners.

Each of these perspectives may be interesting for innovation theology to explore at some point. However, when it comes to the notion of ownership—that which underlies the legal doctrine of limited liability—theology has a distinctly different point of view.

Admittedly the "company of God" is a metaphor and, as with most metaphors, truth happens where the metaphor breaks down, especially in regards to ownership or "controlling interest." With this metaphor there are at least two places where the metaphor breaks to reveal a bit of truth.

The first break in the metaphor has to do with the legal doctrine of limited liability. It's an idea that has to do with limiting the risk of owners. Whether small or large, independent or dependent divisions of a larger corporation, most companies enjoy the privilege and legal right to limit the liability of their owners or shareholders.

This legal invention doesn't appear to be the case for the company of God. Quite the contrary, the company of God has no need for such a limit. It is quite possible that the company of God carries no liability, at least to its major shareholder. It may be, for God, just equity.

The second break in the metaphor is perhaps more of a prophetic critique of common corporate practice. This is the inclination of many company founders to plot their exit strategy. An exit strategy[2] has to do with the sale of the business or, more delicately put, the transfer of ownership. Typically "exit strategy" assumes a transaction wherein owners of the

---

2. "Exit strategy" is also an expression used in the military strategy which is understood as an explicit plan to minimize losses of lives and material (see *Wikipedia*, s.v. "exit strategy").

company give up their full or partial ownership in exchange for cash. When a company is formed with an exit strategy, it reflects a fundamentally different mind-set on the part of the owners from a mind-set of owners who do not anticipate such a transaction.[3]

For God and God's company there is no exit strategy, no final liquidity event.[4] The end is not a transaction or a removal of owner's equity. There seems to be a succession plan, to be sure, but in the company of God success may be viewed less a result and more an event in a succession of events. In other words, unlike many other companies, the company of God appears to be in business for keeps. This has direct bearing on innovating.

Initiating an entrepreneurial start up or innovation effort with at least one eye on the exit is inherently disingenuous. Creating new value for others while simultaneously planning the escape route, or starting a company with the objective of selling out discredits the effort and distorts the purpose of a company—to create and serve a customer with value.[5] Plotting the exit strategy, especially *during* the entrance, does little to engender confidence necessary to catalyze a willingness of others to commit.

Exit strategies unavoidably reveal transactional mind-sets where what owners get is the significant, if not primary, concern. Entrance (or innovation) strategies, on the other hand, tend to come from relational mind-sets, where the purpose of the company is not only to create new value for others but to create customers and serve them. In commercial organizations these two mind-sets—the transactional and the relational—must be maintained in some kind of balance to be sure. But the balance must inexorably tip toward the relational and generous when creating value for another. Transactional and exit strategies retard the generosity, trust and forgiveness required for sustained relationships. Something is missing when our only rationale for investing is simply what we will get in return.

Isn't there another rationale for investing in innovation? Might it be for the chance to leave the social spaces, physical places and people who inhabit them a little better than we found them? This is the kind of question an innovation theology asks, a question that may not otherwise even surface without a theological perspective, and perhaps without the company of God.

---

3. Erickson, *Raising the Bar*, 2–27. Gary recounts his eleventh hour, near "death" experience with an exit he ultimately chose not to take.

4. God's commitment to Noah (and to us) is that there will not be another "liquidity" event (Gen 8:20–22).

5. Drucker, *Management*, 61.

Responding to change *with* the counsel of others is prudent, even when we may seemingly be the only one affected. Responding to change is dangerous when done alone. So is innovating. It is also unnecessary. Counsel from a wise and trusted other is typically a good idea. "Fools think their own way is right, but the wise listen to advice."[6] Keeping our own counsel increases the likelihood that what we imagine to be a response is really a reaction. Alone we are more vulnerable to all sorts of self-justifications. Such justifications are not as easily forthcoming with the counsel of another.

Responding to change *in* the company of others is a bit more complex. Whether family members, coworkers, fellow volunteers or members in common cause, responding to change with others presents a host of other things to consider. Responding to change in the company of others inescapably involves social realities, whether our present company chooses to resist, embrace, adapt or create new value. With social realities come both political and moral ones. And when the company with whom we are responding is a commercial concern it will necessarily involve economic realities as well. But being a part and member of that company—regardless of the company—implies obligation along with affiliation. It does not absolve us of our individual responsibilities

Responding to change *in the company of God*, however, may be another matter entirely. Surprisingly, it may bring us a whole new set of resources, perspectives and even colleagues. Perhaps these have been there all along and we just didn't see them. But when in the company of God, this new set is brought near, expanded potential is freshly awakened. Some call this hope. Others call it encouragement. But whatever we call it, responding to change in the company of God brings confidence to otherwise daunting, complex and uncertain contexts of change.

Responding in the company of God does not imply that we are no longer in the company of others. Quite the opposite is the case. All the various social, moral, political and economic realities remain. In the company of God, however, we have the advantage of a plumb line to direct and guide choices that affect the bottom line. In the company of God we also are more likely to experience the presence, purpose and animating power of God who can do for us what we cannot do for ourselves.

Using "the company of God" as a surrogate for the kingdom of God on earth doesn't lessen or resolve the ambiguities left to us in the words "company" or "kingdom." Both exhibit many of the same ambiguities carried by

6. Prov 12:15; also 11:14; 15:22.

other words used to describe the ways humans associate with each other. Organizations, ventures, initiatives, communities, institutions, enterprises, businesses, the list could go on. All share with "company," however, the notion of human beings associating with each other for some shared purpose, however well or poorly defined.

We might be able to locate and even describe a specific company but *defining* what every company actually is in a standard way may be an impossible task. The impossibility of defining "company" in a consistent and meaningful way may itself be worth noting. But the expression "the company of God" differentiates the interests and orientation of this company from those of others.

Discerning the differences is both necessary and useful, particularly if we are aware of the influence God's plumb line[7] has on our bottom lines. It is only our tendency to compartmentalize the religious from the political, the spiritual from the material, and matters of the soul from matters of the household and societal economy, that prevents us from seeing clearly the purposes and presence of this company of God. Using the phrase "company of God" may point to a significantly different company compared to other companies. But it is still a company.

As a surrogate expression for the kingdom of God on earth, "the company of God" is merely a metaphor. But metaphors bring new insights, broader understandings, and extensions of scope and significance. They can create new space to explore implications that may otherwise go unexplored and unexamined. Such is the intent here. For the metaphor to be effective, however, it should be grounded in the realities it intends to broaden, extend and deepen.[8] To better understand the nature of these realities, therefore, we must first be clear about the meaning of "the kingdom of God."

7. Amos 7:7–8.

8. Perrin, *Rediscovering the Teachings of Jesus*, 87n1.

THE KINGDOM OF GOD[9]

The preponderance of biblical occurrences of the phrase "the kingdom of God"[10] are in the New Testament,[11] primarily in the gospels of Matthew, Mark and Luke. The phrase represents the over-arching and central message of Jesus before and after the resurrection. Regarding this there is widespread agreement among New Testament scholars.

What the phrase actually means, however, garners considerably less consensus among the same scholars. Is it a vision for the future, a present reality, or both? Is it a spiritual phenomenon that transforms the lives of individuals, a socioeconomic dynamic that radically reorders society, or both? Is it a gift that is received, a territory that is entered, or both? Can we describe it only by saying what it is not, or only approximate its meaning through parables with elusive and ambiguous interpretations? Must we accept that it will remain a mystery, at least in part, acknowledging it is not for us to know its times or manifestations?[12] And if it must remain a mystery, then are we for whom it is a mystery, somehow locked out of the kingdom regardless of how much we seek it?

Many of us who pray the way Jesus taught us to pray make an assumption about the kingdom of God. This assumption, often subconsciously held, shows up in the first request of the Lord's Prayer: "Thy kingdom come, thy will be done."[13] The tacit assumption becomes more explicit in what comes next: "on earth as it is in heaven." The assumption is that there is a gap between heaven and earth, between the will of God and the realities of our experience. The good news is that this gap can be closed, and in fact, *is being* closed, no matter what the evidence otherwise seems to suggest. In closing the gap the prayer asks for heavenly realities to shape earthly realities, not the other way around.

---

9. Including the various other interchangeable expressions or translations for the biblical concept of the kingdom of God (e.g., "reign of God" or "kingdom of heaven," the latter of which is a favorite of the Gospel of Matthew).

10. "Kingdom of God" is also understood as "kingdom of heaven" (especially in Matthew's gospel) and "reign of God."

11. Though the phrase and/or concept is not absent in the Hebrew Scriptures; Selman, "Kingdom of God," 161–83.

12. Matt 24:36, 42; 25:13; Mark 13:32–37; Acts 1:6.

13. Matt 6:5–15, esp. v. 10. "Kingdom" and "will" are likely synonymous, at least in the prayer's expression, given the parallelism that saturates prophetic oracles and the Psalms.

This is such a familiar prayer to us that we can often miss the implications. If we pause, however, to consider that for which we are praying, it strikes me that it is perhaps one of the boldest prayers we could pray. It is essentially asking for heaven to manifest itself on earth.

This is an impossible task for humans but not an impossible one for God. It has been said of prayer that it doesn't change God so much as it changes us.[14] Perhaps the question for each of us is whether we see ourselves working for the kingdom of God or for some other kingdom, including perhaps our own? Or is our only question what must I do to guarantee a room reservation for myself in the kingdom of God not on this earth but in heaven, not in this time but in the next?[15]

The good but challenging news about the kingdom of God is that to hold a room reservation for the kingdom in a next life we must participate in the kingdom of God in this life. Regardless of what you and I might anticipate in the next life, this life still requires our time and attention with all its very worldly, messy, imperfect, uncertain and complex circumstances. Here and now God is still active and engaged and "on earth as it is in heaven" is where the company of God operates. Its purpose is to close the gap between heaven and earth.

Much of the debate among scholars regarding the meaning of the kingdom of God has historically centered around its timing. The kingdom of God is thought of as a past memory, a present reality or a future hope. There is plenty of biblical evidence for each of the three. Holding all three simultaneously, however, is difficult to say the least. When the past dominates our understanding of the concept, the kingdom of God points to the restoration of ancient traditions. When the future dominates, the kingdom of God suggests a future hope for individual salvation, societal justice or both. When the present presides, however, the kingdom of God suggests the presence and activity of God—God's current interests, engagements and interventions in the affairs of humankind.

It is this last one—the kingdom of God in the present—that likely holds the most interest for innovation theology. Why? Responding to change is something that happens in the here and now. When that response intends to create new value for others it may be realized in the future but

14. "I pray because I can't help myself. I pray because I'm helpless. I pray because the need flows out of me all the time—waking and sleeping. It doesn't change God—it changes me" (C. S. Lewis, as quoted in the film *Shadowlands*).

15. Matt 19:16–30; Mark 10:17–31; Luke 18:18–30.

the effort it requires is in the present. Innovating may have a mind for the future and certainly an appreciation of the past, but its activity is centered in the here and now.

The kingdom of God *on earth* carries an inherent interest in closing the gap between heaven and earth. Innovating is similarly interested, or at least could and should be. As a result, innovation theology as an applied theology will likely have more interest in the present, "at hand" and "among you" aspects of the kingdom of God, if only because innovating happens in the present tense.

If we bring forward only those biblical references to the kingdom of God that are not explicitly oriented to the future, only those situated more clearly in the present, what we find are several attributes that not only have to do with the company of God, but hold guidance and direction relevant to innovating.

THE KINGDOM ON EARTH

A thorough and complete exegesis of all these "present oriented"[16] references is beyond the scope of this essay and likely the competence of the author. Indeed, the present orientation of the kingdom of God can confound even the best. Consider when Jesus was asked by the Pharisees about when the kingdom of God was coming, he answered, "The kingdom of God is not coming with things that can be observed; nor will they say, 'Look, here it is!' or 'There it is!' For, in fact, the kingdom of God is among you."[17] Clearly, the kingdom of God in the now is not self-evident to all.

However, these present oriented references point directly to a few distinguishing characteristics, which when combined, make this kingdom different from any and all other human kingdoms. These characteristics include the present kingdom's bias for *persons in need, forgiveness extended, local commitment, participation more than outcomes,* and *serving not status.* These are the who, how, where and why of the kingdom of God on earth. Take a brief look at each of these.

---

16. Some of the kingdom of God references are oriented to the future, others to the present. To see the difference, compare the parable (and Jesus' explanation) of the sower and the seeds (Matt 13:1–9 explained in 13:18–23) and the parable of the weeds among the wheat (Matt 13:24–30 explained in 13:36–43).

17. Luke 17:20–21.

Persons in need. In the Beatitudes[18]—arguably a diagnostic for the kingdom of God on earth—Jesus says that the kingdom of God belongs to the poor in spirit and to those who are persecuted for righteousness' sake. Because these two Beatitudes are the first and last in the set of eight, we can reasonably infer the kingdom of God belongs to those named in the other six—those who mourn, the meek, those who hunger and thirst for righteousness, the merciful, the pure in heart and the peacemakers.

All of these are persons in need. In fact, it may be appropriate to infer that the kingdom of God on earth is not only *for* persons in need but *among* persons in need. Those who have been transformed by loss or longing can be more acutely aware of their own powerlessness. As a result, they are better positioned to see and understand the new value that can be created for others, particularly others in need. Isn't this experience-born empathy what distinguishes sacrificial love (*agape*) from other kinds of love?[19]

This inference aligns with Jesus' designation of those to whom he thought he was especially sent[20]—the poor, the captives, the blind, and the oppressed. Likewise, when the disciples of John the Baptist come to Jesus to ask him, "Are you the one who is to come or are we to wait for another?" Jesus replies, "Go and tell John what you have seen and heard: the blind receive their sight, the lame walk, the lepers are cleansed, the deaf hear, the dead are raised, (and) the poor have good news brought to them."[21]

The kingdom of God on earth has a bias for persons in need, the marginalized, poor and oppressed; the lost and those who have lost.

Forgiveness extended. Peter asks how often forgiveness should be extended.[22] Jesus famously replies, "Not even seven times, but seventy times seven." Then Jesus compares the kingdom of God to a king who wished to settle accounts with his slaves to explain this forgiveness strategy.[23]

In the parable the king shows compassion and forgives the one who owes a considerable sum but cannot repay it. The king's forgiveness comes only after the debtor acknowledges the dire consequences of his inability to repay the debt. This debtor, however, turns right around and demands

---

18. Matt 5:3–10.

19. Lewis, *Four Loves*.

20. Luke 4:18–19. As Jesus is quoting Isa 61:1–2, the list of certain persons in Isaiah is similar: the oppressed, the brokenhearted, captives, prisoners and all who mourn.

21. Luke 7:21–22.

22. Matt 18:21–22.

23. Matt 18:23–35.

payment from another who owes him considerably less. The contradiction did not escape the notice of others. They bring this to the attention of the king, who calls the forgiven one back in to face the music and fess up.

The parable unambiguously points to an essential characteristic of the kingdom of God on earth—extending to others the forgiveness we have received ourselves. Of course, such forgiveness is hardly extensible without having first received it our selves. But extending forgiveness becomes a challenge when we have either amnesia about the forgiveness we have experienced or transactional proclivities to settle accounts and "reconcile" perhaps even more than the books. Such amnesia causes us to think of ourselves as end points where forgiveness rests, rather than the channels where forgiveness flows. "The kingdom of God is known in terms of the experience of the forgiveness of sins; the only proper response to that experience is a preparedness in turn to forgive."[24]

The kingdom of God on earth has a bias for forgiveness extended.

Local commitment. Jesus' explanation of the parable of the sower and the seeds refers the kingdom of God.[25] Jesus compares the content of the message of the kingdom of God to the seed that is sown on different soils. When sown on the hard, well-trod path, the seed finds no soil at all. It is not understood. When sown in rocky soil, the seed may be received with joy, but it cannot take root. When trouble comes, as it inevitably will, the joy is short lived and what has sprouted falls away. When the seed is sown among thorns—the cares of the world and the lure of wealth—the seed is choked out and it yields nothing. It is only in the good soil—soil wherein the seed can take root—that the seed is able to bear fruit and yield, even exponentially. Seeds are irrelevant unless and until they find soil in which to commit themselves. Local commitment. "Think globally, act locally" may have gotten it right.

The parables of the mustard seed, the yeast, the treasure in the field, and the pearl of great price[26] also speak of this local commitment as part and parcel of the kingdom of God. What each of these parables suggests is that the potential of the kingdom of God, however it is imagined, is irrelevant if it is not planted, if there is "un-hedged" commitment to it.

The kingdom of God on earth has a bias for local commitment, where time, attention and devotion are planted and roots are established.

---

24. Perrin, *Rediscovering the Teachings of Jesus*, 126.

25. Matt 13:19.

26. Matt 13:31–32 (mustard seed), 33 (yeast), 44 (treasure), and 45 (pearls).

Participation more than outcomes. In the instruction set Jesus lays out to the seventy[27] Jesus makes it clear that regardless of the outcomes the seventy are to say at the end of their efforts "The kingdom of God has come near to you." This declaration is to be expressed whether their efforts are received or not. The outcome of their efforts matters, certainly. But the outcome is not the responsibility of the seventy.

Letting go of the outcomes is also inferred in Jesus' counsel to the disciples not to worry—not to strive for what they are to eat or drink—even for the most basic necessities of life. "For it is the nations of the world that strive after all these things, and your Father knows that you need them. Instead, strive for God's kingdom, and these things will be given to you as well."[28] Our part in the kingdom of God on earth is not to worry about the outcomes. Rather, it's about working for the kingdom's purposes.

Perhaps nowhere else is this participation-more-than-outcome emphasis clearer than in the parable Jesus tells about the day laborers.[29] Though hired at different intervals and therefore working different lengths of time, the landowner chooses to pay them all the same amount. Our common sense of fairness is offended by this parable. Yet the parable concludes with the reminder of the absolute freedom of the landowner to do what he chooses with what belongs to him. The chance to participate in the work of the kingdom of God on earth is more important than whatever rewards or results happen come to those who participate.

The kingdom of God on earth has a bias for our participation more than our worry with outcomes.

Serving not status. In a revealing little narrative recorded in the Gospel of Matthew the mother of James and John approaches Jesus to ask for a favor.[30] The favor turns out to be more than a little favor. "Declare that these two sons of mine will sit, one at your right hand and one at your left, in your kingdom." Jesus responds by saying that she has no idea what she is asking, and after a brief exchange, says that such a favor is not his to grant.

This interchange would at first appear to be one of those future oriented references regarding the kingdom of God. But when the other disciples got wind of the mother's request, Jesus took the opportunity to bring it all back to the present, diverting the maternal interest in the future and turning the

27. Luke 10:1–12.
28. Luke 12:30–31.
29. Matt 20:1–16.
30. Matt 20:20–28.

quest for status upside down. "Whoever wishes to be great among you must be your servant, and whoever wishes to be first among you must be your slave; just as the Son of Man came not to be served but to serve."

This interest in serving not status often catches us by surprise. It seems at first counterintuitive, as it did for the disciples who when invited to "come and inherit the kingdom prepared for you from the foundation of the world"[31] asked, "Lord, when was it that we saw you hungry and gave you food, or thirsty and gave you something to drink? And when was it that we saw you a stranger and welcomed you, or naked and gave you clothing? And when was it that we saw you sick or in prison and visited you?" Jesus answers, "As you did it to the least of these, you did it to me."

The kingdom of God on earth clearly has a bias for service not status.

These characteristics of the kingdom of God on earth direct and guide us to what it means to respond to change and to innovate in the company of God. When we are more focused on persons in need than the innovativeness of our solutions, more ready to extend the forgiveness we have received, more willing to commit ourselves locally than achieve scalability, more concerned about the quality of our participation than the quantity of our rewards, and more interested in serving than status, then we may be "not far from the kingdom of God." Could it be that one reason so many innovating efforts end in failure and wasted effort stems from these efforts being otherwise directed?

A word of caution is due here, though. In all our well-intentioned serving, experience-born empathy, local commitment, forgiveness extended and participation, we can so easily forget the fact that God plays the lead. God's leadership is so often missed, partly because God is among us as one who serves while we are looking for God's leadership as one who rules. Isn't God the One whose understanding is unfathomably detailed,[32] who knows needs even before we ask?[33] Isn't it God who animates the growth, who initiates the forgiveness, who takes special care for persons in need, who commits locally before we do? Isn't it God who looks after the outcomes, in part, so that we might be freed to concentrate on the inputs?

If these are the distinguishing realities of the kingdom of God on earth—God's engaged, active presence—they do not necessarily make the expression "the company of God" the *only* surrogate. These realities,

31. Matt 25:31–46.

32. Ps 139.

33. Matt 6:8.

however, provide direction for the task of innovation theology, to which we now turn our attention.

RELEVANCE FOR INNOVATION THEOLOGY

If the expression "company of God" finds acceptance, its utility will not likely be found in any reform of theology, per se. Rather, the value of the expression may more likely reside in its inherent prophetic challenge for companies and their leaders to carefully consider where and why innovations are needed.

Aligning our innovating efforts with the purposes of God's company gets us closer to doing what we are designed to do—work toward closing the gap between heaven and earth. It also promises a purposefulness, satisfaction and sense of fulfillment that is not possible nor as authentic or satisfying from any other "returns" for which we may otherwise invest ourselves. Aligning ourselves with the company of God in order to increase the probability of success in innovating is highly susceptible to self-justification and all manner of self-delusion. It's also adolescent theology.

Historically, companies have proven more responsive to change than any other organizational form. Companies are more adaptive and malleable. Companies have proven certainly more responsive than kingdoms. Castles are the legacy of monarchs and their reigns. Old forts with massive defenses still stand despite the fact that there is no longer anything against which to defend. They have become museums. The nature and character of such adaptive capability, and God's interest in it, will likely prove of significant interest to innovation theology, largely because adaptive capability represents greater potential for responding to change and may be the most important capability a company intending to innovate can have.[34]

An early example of this adaptive capability was in the company of Francesco di Marco Datini. Datini was born in Prato, Italy in 1335. After starting his company under the banner "For God and Profit" in Avignon, he returned to Prato where he set up over three hundred different partnerships operating in a variety of different businesses, from retail shops to textiles and jewelry and even banking. Datini was convinced that being in *campaigne* (in company) with others just made better business sense than operating alone. Datini became known as "The Merchant of Prato," a recognized success largely based on his ability to "keep things as loose and flexible as possible."[35]

---

34. Teece, "Dynamic Capabilities," 509–33.

35. Micklethwait and Wooldridge, *Company*, 11.

Datini knew then what many have emulated since. Companies carry greater responsive and adaptive potential. In fact, the influence, effectiveness and adaptability of companies led John Micklethwait and Adrian Wooldridge to observe:

> Hegel predicted that the basic unit of modern society would be the state, Marx that it would be the commune, Lenin and Hitler that it would be the political party. Before that, a succession of saints and sages claimed the same for the parish church, the feudal manor, and the monarchy. . . . They all have been proved wrong. The most important organization in the world is the company: the basis of the prosperity of the West and the best hope for the future of the rest of the world.[36]

Perhaps this applies even more so to the company of God.

Before we get carried away with the potential of companies, however, we should consider the company's relationship with the state. Companies have seemingly always had uneasy relations with nation states, from which these companies obtain their rights to exist and operate. The unease between the two might be due in part to the greater willingness and ability of companies to adapt and respond to change than their slower, more plodding peers among institutions with ruling and regulating authority. That God might choose to use both—the responsive, adaptive company and the regulatory, governing institution—for the purposes of God's company is certainly well within the scope of God's choice. Nor is such a choice without biblical precedent.

One of the more remarkable passages of Scripture is Isaiah's short oracle of eight verses that names Cyrus as God's own *anointed*.[37] Not only is Cyrus not an Israelite. He is not even from traceable descendents of Abraham. He's a completely secular figure, a Persian King. But none of this prevents God from commissioning Cyrus to be an instrument of the company of God. And just to be sure there is no doubt about who does the anointing, God uses the first person pronoun no less than fourteen times:

> . . . whose right hand I have grasped . . .
>
> I will go before you . . .
>
> I will break in pieces the doors of bronze
>
> I will give you the treasures of darkness

36. Ibid., xv.

37. *Anointed* means "messiah," or in the New Testament "Christ."

... so that you may know that it is I, ... who calls you by name ...
I surname you, though you do not know me,
I am the Lord ...
I arm you, though you do not know me ...
I am the Lord, and there is no other.
I form light and create darkness,
I make weal and create woe;
I the Lord do all these things.
... I the Lord have create it.[38]

Another remarkable passage points to the same divine operation. It is also outside the conventional boundaries to which we typically confine the company of God. It is Jesus' recognition of faith on the part of the Roman Centurion. Like Cyrus, here is another, a complete outsider, of whom Jesus was amazed and said, "I tell you, not even in Israel have I found such faith."[39]

We typically want to contain and limit the purposes of God. But Scripture, Jesus and God will not let us. God always looks well beyond the beloved community.[40] Why should we imagine that God might refrain from using secular companies—whether sprawling global corporations, midsize organizations or even small, family companies—to use as instruments of God's purpose, if God so chooses?

The company of God, descriptively at least, reflects the freedom of God. This freedom includes the freedom to reconfigure, adapt and form relationships with whomever and whatever God so chooses. The company of God is quite capable of making acquisitions of other companies, even without the awareness of the acquired. If the acquired company is positioned to serve the purposes of the company of God, who are we to say that the acquired must consciously agree, much less even be aware of the divine acquisition?

Who and what is acquired—individuals, other companies and organizations, even nations—can be transformed in the process for the purposes of the company of God. Such acquisitions, or divestments, are the choice of the Acquirer more than the choice of the acquired. In fact, if it were possible for the acquired to control or orchestrate the acquisition we would likely have the dangerous situation where those who believe they are acting

38. Isa 45:1–8; see also Childs, *Isaiah*, 353–54; and Brueggemann, *Isaiah*, 40–66, 75–76.

39. Luke 7:1–10; Matt 8:5–13.

40. Brueggemann, *Isaiah*, 76.

on behalf of God risk self-justification, not to mention self-righteousness. Self-assurance that one is operating in the company of God may itself be a sign of the opposite.

This adaptive, adoptive and even acquisitive freedom of God's company—arguably a derivative aspect of God's sovereignty—suggests a concept of ownership very different from what we normally think of as ownership. God's ownership (inferred from his authorship[41] as the creator) and our conceptions of ownership, rooted as they are in John Locke's notion of the natural right of property, are quite different. This makes it a bit difficult to wrap our minds around the practical implications of God's ownership,[42] in contrast to the ownership of company assets, tangible or intangible.[43]

However, this much can be said. God's ownership is more a matter of the free and purposeful intention of the Author to do with as God's chooses than it is about proprietary "rights" of the divine. I suspect that God is not too concerned with God's rights. *We* may choose to transfer and assign ownership rights to others with what we believe (mistakenly or not) that we own. But I don't believe that God gives up, assigns or transfers God's ownership "rights" (or responsibilities) to others. Stewardship is the *delegation* of management responsibility, not ownership.

Notwithstanding the Fall, God's original intention seemed to be to put us in the garden to "till it and to keep it,"[44] not own it. As Gerhard von Rad put it: "That [mankind] was transferred to the garden to guard it indicates that he was called to a state of service and had to prove himself in a realm that was not his own possession."[45]

The concept of a company carries a strong preference for a sense-and-respond orientation compared to the command-and-control orientation associated with "kingdom." And while a command-and-control mind-set

---

41. While "authorship" may be similar to ownership there are some significant differences that may be worth exploring for innovation theology, given the importance of intellectual property (i.e., inventorship with patents and authorship with copyrights) for so many companies.

42. Exod 19:5; Ps 24:1; 95:5; Ezek 18:4.

43. Given that 75 percent or more of market capitalization of publicly traded companies is now based on intangible assets vs. tangible or "book value," the intellectual property these assets represent and their influence on innovating is worth exploring theologically, though beyond the scope of this essay (see Blair, *Unseen Wealth*).

44. Gen 2:15.

45. von Rad, *Genesis*, 80.

may be appropriate and even necessary for managing and running existing operations, it is disastrous for responding to change and innovating.

Companies that respond to change and innovate faster and better than their peers have done so in large measure due to their capability to sense-and-respond. "Throughout its history, the company has shown an equally remarkable ability to evolve: indeed, that has been the secret of its success."[46] More than any other institution or organization, companies have learned to respond to change and innovate faster and better. This does not imply that all companies have learned to do this. Those that have not tend to be short lived. Neither does it imply that their greater responsiveness to change means the company will achieve a longer life than its peers who suffer from learning disabilities.[47] Rather, it is simply implying that there are no other socioeconomic architectures better suited to responding to change and innovating than the company.[48] Kingdoms are simply slower to respond and adapt.

"Company" doesn't *necessarily* imply this sense-and-respond mindset. There are plenty of declining companies who have lost their way regardless of their relative or current state of profitability. Many of these are well along the path of decline, having lost a sense of their own entrepreneurial vocation, or having allowed their core competences to drift into core rigidities.[49] To be fair, neither "company" nor "kingdom" is likely the perfect metaphorical carrier of the purpose and presence of God. But "company" certainly holds a more relevant frame for responding to change and innovating because of this stronger association with sense-and-respond.

Most adaptive systems, those that sense-and-respond, are able to do so effectively because they have a center point that enables them to maintain their balance, like the keel of a sailboat. The ability to sense-and-respond stems from the ability to sense and make sense of what is going on amidst the winds of change blowing through the immediate environment. It comes, in part, from having a sufficiently strong and coherent sense of purpose or direction.

The keel in a company is its purpose or reason for being. "A reason for being expresses essential organizational purpose. It states what the organization

46. Micklethwait and Wooldridge, *Company*, 181.

47. Geus, *Living Company*, vii.

48. Some might suggest that the "network" represents a viable alternative social architecture. However, networks have neither the internal system of accountabilities (see Micklethwait and Woolridge, *Company*, 184), nor the focus of purposeful action that companies do.

49. Leonard-Barton, "Core Capabilities," 111–25.

exists to do, as opposed to what it must do to exist."[50] The command-and-control of kingdoms tends to rely on planning and assumes a much higher degree of control than either reality or change actually affords. "Planned responses do not work,"[51] especially in highly uncertain and unpredictable environments. More important than planning is "the ability to transform apparent noise into meaning faster than apparent noise" is received.

> Sense-and-respond organizations leverage this insight into a generic way of fostering adaptive sense-making and action. The particulars of what is sensed and of how it is interpreted are role-specific (and purpose-specific) and depend on the amount of adaptability required.[52]

The way to turn noise into signal and signal into meaning is to be clear on what one's purpose is, as an individual or an organization. In the company of God this purpose is clear, despite our propensity to muddle it up. That the company of God has no exit strategy does not imply that it has no strategy or purpose at all. Its strategy, if we can infer it from Jesus' own understanding of his purpose, is the same as the strategy of the kingdom of God on earth:

> The spirit of the Lord God is upon me,
> because the Lord has anointed me; he has sent me
> to bring good news to the oppressed,
> to bind up the broken-hearted,
> to proclaim liberty to the captives, and release to the prisoners;
> to proclaim the year of the Lord's favor, and the day of vengeance of our God;
> to comfort all who mourn.[53]

With such a clear sense of purpose, any individual or organization is freed to sense what is happening in the environment, make sense and respond in a way that is true to that purpose *and* the (new) sense it can make of its environment. In such sense-and-respond mind-sets there is a greater bias for what is voluntary, compared to what is compelled or coerced, for what is done out of a generous spirit compared to a transactional one, for

---

50. Haeckel, *Adaptive Enterprise*, 114.

51. Ibid., xvii.

52. Ibid., xviii (parentheses mine).

53. Isa 61:1–2; see also Luke 4:18–19, wherein Jesus adds "recovery of sight to the blind."

what is born out of trust than specified in legal contracts, and for risks worth taking more than liabilities worth limiting.

Saying that the company of God is more sense-and-respond oriented than command-and-control oriented might suggest a God that is more interested in responsiveness than in stability or consistency. Depending upon one's reading of the Old Testament saga of God's dealings with the people of Israel, this could be a reasonable conclusion. The God of the Old Testament is anything but monochromatic and monosyllabic, much less static.

CONCLUSION

Why consider a surrogate for the kingdom of God on earth? Why not stick with the phrase as it is? After all, it's a phrase that saturates the Gospels of Matthew, Mark and Luke, and shows up in some noteworthy places in the rest of the New Testament. The answer is quite simple and pragmatic. "The company of God" resonates better with contexts of responding to change and innovating.

The prophet Samuel was particularly sensitive to this, despite being overruled by God. In that debate between Samuel and God about the whole king and kingdom idea,[54] Samuel was clearly of the opinion that it was a bad idea. Samuel thought it was better to not overthink or overorganize. Besides, the people wanted a king because their neighbors all seemed to have one.

Perhaps Samuel might have preferred the alternative of a company, had it been available to his imagination. At least it might have avoided the risk associated with so many sovereigns. Or perhaps Samuel's parting counsel is as relevant to companies today as it was to the fledgling young kingdom then:

> If you will fear the Lord and serve him and heed his voice and not rebel against the commandment of the Lord, and if both you and the king who reigns over you will follow the Lord your God, it will be well; but if you will not heed the voice of the Lord, but rebel against the commandment of the Lord, then the hand of the Lord will be against you and your king.[55]

Being invited into an innovating, responsive and global company with one sustaining purpose, an eternal, ongoing purpose that is greater than any other company's purpose, is really good news. We should get to

54. 1 Sam 8–16.

55. 1 Sam 12:14–16.

know more about this company and its purpose of closing the gap between heaven and earth.

Certainly more about the company of God can and should be explored in succeeding conversations about innovation theology. And whether the phrase sticks or we return to the workable but slightly longer "the kingdom of God on earth," the exploration of its purpose will be especially important for directing and guiding society in its response to change and where and why innovations are needed.

For now, however, it may be enough to at least point to where the phrase "the company of God" represents its counterpart in the biblical vocabulary. More importantly it likely suggests how being a participant *in* this company, "in Christ" to use Paul's phrase, might help close the gaps between heaven and earth for all of us, and help us avoid the various idols, illusions and delusions of the kingdoms and companies of mankind.

Where to From Here?

A SINGLE NOTION AND affirmation saturates the preceding: God is both interested and invested in innovation. To express this in a more imperative manner: the One for whom all things are possible continues to invite us to co-create new value for others in the company of God.

If there is any truth to this, the entrepreneurially active might want to consider engaging in conversations with the theologically curious. Such conversations might make further explorations and chart the largely unexplored territory of innovation theology. In this wilderness there will likely be some wandering, a little whining, but also a lot of wondering, all of which promise more substantive and sustainable innovating.

Specifically, institutions of theological education might want to become sponsors and hosts of such conversations. As hosts, invitations will need to be sent out to others beyond the institution's familiar boundaries. Those on the invitation list will necessarily include innovators, economists, technologists and others who are entrepreneurially inclined, though themselves theologically curious. Identifying these participants may take some effort, but may also be easier than we might at first imagine. Those already engaged in charting where theology intersects with the dynamics of contemporary culture, the marketplace and leadership may be the most likely participants for sponsors and hosts.

Given the other things on the short list of priorities for schools of theology these days, innovation theology may not make it to the top on its own. However, responding to change with the aim of creating new value for others may be refreshingly relevant to the existing items already atop those lists; items like social and economic justice, the stewardship of creation, truth and reconciliation, or the recovery of individuals and organizations who have lost their way, even the growing numbers who check the box "none" for religious affiliation. In fact, innovating may be more resonant with what we typically think it means to till and keep[1] the garden God has given us, or to being our brother's and sister's keeper.[2]

Based on this simple affirmation, this primer on innovation theology has tried to offer a non-obvious but bold proposal: that biblical theology has something both meaningful and practical to contribute to innovating. Whether this proposal meets with consideration or not, the occurrence, character and content of conversations regarding innovation theology will bear witness. Time will tell.

In the meantime, change keeps changing, and God—a living, loving and unbelievably patient God—keeps inviting us through change to respond. We can react or we can respond. This choice seems constant.

If we choose to respond rather than react, then we have another choice to make—whether our response will aim to create new value for others in the company of God, or seek refuge and extend for as long as possible what appears to be familiar, safe and even secure, in our own company. Innovation theology can and should help us to see, make sense of, believe and even make the right choice.

1. Gen 2:15.
2. Gen 4:9.

Bibliography

Ackoff, Russell L. *Differences That Make a Difference*. Axminster, UK: Triarchy, 2010.

———. "From Data to Wisdom." *Journal of Applied Systems Analysis* 16 (1989) 59–70.

———. *Re-Creating the Corporation: A Design of Organizations for the 21st Century*. New York: Oxford University Press, 1999.

Ackoff, Russell L., and Fred E. Emery. *On Purposeful Systems: An Interdisciplinary Analysis of Individual and Social Behavior as a System of Purposeful Events*. New Brunswick: Transaction, 1972.

Aeppel, Timothy. "Why Is Productivity Slowing Down?" *Wall Street Journal*, January 28, 2013.

Australian Public Service Commission. "Tackling Wicked Problems: A Public Policy Perspective." October 25, 2007.

Blair, Margaret. *Unseen Wealth: Report of the Brookings Task Force on Intangibles*. Washington, DC: Brookings Institution Press, 2001.

Blomberg, Craig L. *Neither Poverty Nor Riches: A Biblical Theology of Possessions*. Downers Grove: InterVarsity, 1999.

Bouderi, Robert. *Engines of Tomorrow: How the World's Best Companies Are Using Their Research Labs to Win the Future*. New York: Simon & Schuster, 2000.

Bovon, Francois. *Luke 2: A Commentary on the Gospel of Luke 9:51—19:27*. Translated by Donald S. Deer. Minneapolis: Fortress, 2013.

Brown, Leslie, ed. *The New Shorter Oxford English Dictionary*. 2 vols. Oxford: Clarendon, 1993.

Brown, Stuart. *Play: How It Shapes the Brain, Opens the Imagination, and Invigorates the Soul*. With Christopher Vaughan. New York: Penguin, 2009.

Brueggemann, Walter. *Isaiah 1–39*. Louisville: Westminster John Knox, 1998.

———. *The Practice of Prophetic Imagination: Preaching an Emancipating Word*. Minneapolis: Fortress, 2012.

———. *The Prophetic Imagination*. Minneapolis: Fortress, 2001.

———. *Reality, Grief, Hope: Three Urgent Prophetic Tasks*. Grand Rapids: Eerdmans, 2014.

———. *Remember You Are Dust*. Eugene: Wipf & Stock, 2012.

Buechner, Frederick. *Telling the Truth: Gospel as Tragedy, Comedy and Fairy Tale.* New York: Harper & Row, 1977.

Calvin, Jean. *The Institutes of the Christian Religion.* Edited by John T. McNeill. Translated by Ford Lewis Battles. 2 vols. Philadelphia: Westminster, 1975.

Cameron, Doug, and Julian E. Barnes. "Pentagon Presses Contractors to Innovate." *Wall Street Journal,* November 20, 2014. http://online.wsj.com/articles/pentagon-to-defense-contractors-innovate-1416527136.

Carr, Herbert Wildon. *Henri Bergson: The Philosopher of Change.* London: Elibron Classics, 2004.

Chase, Alston. *In a Dark Wood: The Fight over the Forests and the Myths of Nature.* New Brunswick, NJ: Transaction, 2001.

Cheverton, Richard. *The Maverick Way: Profiting from the Power of the Corporate Misfit.* Costa Mesa, CA: Maverwickway.com, 2000.

Childs, Brevard S. *Biblical Theology of the Old and New Testaments: Theological Reflection on the Christian Bible.* Minneapolis: Fortress, 2011. First published 1992.

———. *Isaiah.* Louisville: Westminster John Knox, 2001.

———. *The New Testament as Canon: An Introduction.* Philadelphia: Fortress, 1984.

Christensen, Clayton M. *The Innovator's Dilemma: When New Technologies Cause Great Firms to Fail.* Boston: Harvard Business School Press, 1997.

Christensen, Clayton M., and Michael E. Raynor. *The Innovator's Solution: Creating and Sustaining Successful Growth.* Boston: Harvard Business School Press, 2003.

Christensen, Clayton M., and Derek van Bever. "The Capitalist's Dilemma." *Harvard Business Review,* June 2014. https://hbr.org/2014/06/the-capitalists-dilemma.

Collins, Jim. *How the Mighty Fall and Why Some Companies Never Give In.* New York: HarperCollins, 2009.

Cox, Harvey. *The Future of Faith.* New York: HarperCollins, 2009.

Csikszentmihalyi, Mihaly. *Creativity: The Psychology of Discovery and Invention.* New York: HarperCollins, 1996.

Daly, Herman E. *Beyond Growth: The Economics of Sustainable Development.* Boston: Beacon, 1996.

———. *Steady-State Economics.* 2nd ed. Washington, DC: Island, 1991.

Daly, Herman E., and John B. Cobb. *For the Common Good: Redirecting the Economy toward Community, the Environment and a Sustainable Future.* Boston: Beacon, 1994. First published 1989.

Davenport, Thomas H., and John C. Beck. *The Attention Economy: Understanding the New Currency of Business.* Boston: Harvard Business School Press, 2001.

Denning, Steve. "The Surprising Reasons Why American Lost Its Ability to Compete." *Forbes.com,* March 10, 2013. http://www.forbes.com/sites/stevedenning/2013/03/10/the-surprising-reasons-why-america-lost-its-ability-to-compete.

Drucker, Peter. *The Ecological Vision: Reflections on the American Condition.* New Brunswick: Transaction, 2001.

———. *Innovation and Entrepreneurship: Practice and Principles.* New York: Harper & Row, 1985.

———. *Management: Tasks, Responsibilities and Practices.* New York: Harper & Row, 1974.

Dukas, Helen, and Banesh Hoffmann, eds. *Albert Einstein, the Human Side: New Glimpses from His Archives.* Princeton: Princeton University Press, 1979.

Dweck, Carol S. *Mindset: The New Psychology of Success.* New York: Ballantine, 2006.

Erickson, Gary. *Raising the Bar: Integrity and Passion in Life and Business*. San Francisco: Jossey-Bass, 2004.

Foster, Richard. *Innovation: The Attacker's Advantage*. New York: Summit, 1986.

Frankl, Viktor E. *Man's Search for Meaning*. New York: Washington Square, 1984.

Friedman, Edwin H. *A Failure of Nerve: Leadership in the Age of the Quick Fix*. New York: Seabury, 2007. First published 1999.

———. *Generation to Generation: Family Process in Church and Synagogue*. New York: Guilford, 1985.

Geus, Arie de. *The Living Company: Habits for Survival in a Turbulent Business Environment*. Boston: Harvard Business School Press, 1997.

Gilding, Paul. *The Great Disruption: Why the Climate Crisis Will Bring On the End of Shopping and the Birth of a New World*. New York: Bloomsbury, 2011.

Goodchild, Philip. *Theology of Money*. Durham: Duke University Press, 2009.

Gordon, William J. J. *Synectics: The Development of Creative Capacity*. New York: Collier, 1968. First published 1961.

Haeckel, Stephan H. *Adaptive Enterprise*. Boston: Harvard Business School Press, 1999.

Haenchen, Ernst. *John 2: A Commentary on the Gospel of John Chapters 7–21*. Translated by R. W. Funk. Philadelphia: Fortress, 1984.

Hock, Dee. *The Birth of the Chaordic Age*. San Francisco: Berrett-Koehler, 1999.

Horden, William. "Idolatry." In *A Dictionary of Christian Theology*, edited by Alan Richardson, . Philadelphia: Westminster, 1969.

Hunter, James Davison. *To Change the World: The Irony, Tragedy, and Possibility of Christianity in the Late Modern World*. Oxford: Oxford University Press, 2010.

Hyde, Lewis. *The Gift: How the Creative Spirit Transforms the World*. Edinburgh: Canongate, 2007. First published 1983.

Ip, Greg. "The Dangers of Deflation: The Pendulum Swings to the Pit." October 25, 2014. https://gregip.wordpress.com/2014/11/17/the-dangers-of-deflation-the-pendulum-swings-to-the-pit.

Isaacson, Walter. *Einstein: His Life and Universe*. New York: Simon & Schuster, 2007.

Jackson, Tim. *Prosperity Without Growth: Economics for a Finite Planet*. London: Earthscan, 2011.

James, William. *The Varieties of Religious Experience: A Study in Human Nature*. New York: Random House, 2002.

Johansson, Fran. *The Medici Effect: Breakthrough Insights at the Intersection of Ideas, Concepts, and Cultures*. Boston: Harvard Business School Press, 2004.

Jung, Carl G. *Synchronicity*. Princeton: Princeton University Press, 2011. First published 1960.

Kahneman, Daniel. *Thinking, Fast and Slow*. New York: Farrar, Straus and Giroux, 2011.

Kanter, Rosabeth Moss. *The Change Masters: Innovation for Productivity in the American Corporation*. New York: Simon and Schuster, 1983.

Krishnamurti, Jiddu. *The Impossible Question*. http://www.jkrishnamurti.com/krishnamurti-teachings/view-text.php?s=books&tid=9&chid=57009.

Kung, Hans. *The Church*. New York: Sheed and Ward, 1967.

Leonard-Barton, Dorothy. "Core Capabilities and Core Rigidities: A Paradox in Managing New Product Development." Special issue, *Strategic Management Journal* 13 (1992).

Lester, Ricard K., and Michael J. Piore. *Innovation: The Missing Dimension*. Cambridge: Harvard University Press, 2004.

Lewis, C. S. *The Four Loves*. New York: Harcourt, Brace, 1960.

————. *Mere Christianity*. New York: HarperCollins, 2001. First published 1952.

Luther, Martin. *Saemmtliche Schriften*. Edited by Ed Walch. Translated by Erika Bullman Flores. St. Louis: Condordia, 1880–1910.

Magnuson, Stew. "Military 'Swimming in Sensors and Drowning in Data.'" *National Defense*, January 2010. http://www.nationaldefensemagazine.org/archive/2010/January/Pages/Military'SwimmingInSensorsandDrowninginData'.aspx.

Marglin, Stephen A. *The Dismal Science: How Thinking Like an Economist Undermines Community*. Cambridge: Harvard University Press, 2010.

McIntyre, Marilyn. *Caring for Words in the Culture of Lies*. Grand Rapids: Eerdmans, 2009.

Meadows, Donella. *Thinking in Systems: A Primer*. White River Junction, VT: Sustainability Institute, 2008.

Mele, Nicco. *The End of Big: How the Digital Revolution Makes David the New Goliath*. New York: St. Martin's, 2014.

Merhabian, Albert. *Non-verbal Communication*. Chicago: Aldine-Atherton, 1972.

Micklethwait, John, and Adrian Wooldridge. *The Company: A Short History of a Revolutionary Idea*. New York: Random House, 2005.

Moltmann, Jurgen. *The Church in the Power of the Holy Spirit: A Contribution to Messianic Ecclesiology*. New York: Harper & Row, 1977.

Moore, Geoffrey A. *Crossing the Chasm*. New York: HarperBusiness, 1991.

Morath, Eric. "Treasury Secretary Lew Warns of Lower Potential Economic Growth: Congressional Budget Office Projects Average Growth Rate of Just 2.1% Going Forward." *Wall Street Journal*, June 11, 2014.

Morgan, James M., and Jeffrey K. Liker. *The Toyota Product Development System: Integrated People, Process, and Technology*. New York: Productivity, 2006.

Moser, Paul K. *The Elusive God: Reorienting Religious Epistemology*. Cambridge: Cambridge University Press, 2008.

Nicholson, William. *Shadowlands*. New York: Penguin, 1990.

Niebuhr, Reinhold. *Moral Man and Immoral Society: A Study in Ethics and Politics*. New York: Scribner, 1960. First published 1932.

Niebuhr, H. Richard, *Christ and Culture*. New York: Harper & Row, 1951.

————. *The Meaning of Revelation*. New York: Macmillan, 1941.

————. *The Purpose of the Church and Its Ministry*. New York: Harper & Row, 1956.

Nisbett, Richard E. *The Geography of Thought: How Asians and Westerners Think Differently . . . and Why*. New York: Free, 2003.

Nonaka, Ikujiro, and Noboru Konno. "The Concept of Ba: Building a Foundation for Knowledge Creation." *California Management Review* 40 (1998) 40–54.

Nonaka, Ikujiro, and Hirotaka Takeuchi. *The Knowledge-Creating Company: How Japanese Companies Create the Dynamics of Innovation*. New York: Oxford University Press, 1995.

Ong, Walter J. *Orality and Literacy: The Technologizing of the Word*. London: Routledge, 2002. First published 1982.

Packard, David. *The HP Way: How Bill Hewlett and I Built Our Company*. New York: HarperCollins, 1995.

Paley, William. *Natural Theology or Evidences of the Existence and Attributes of the Deity*. London, 1802.

Palmisano, Sam. "Managing Investors." Interview by the *Harvard Business Review*, June 2014. https://hbr.org/2014/06/managing-investors.

Perrin, Norman. *Rediscovering the Teachings of Jesus*. New York: Harper & Row, 1967.

Piattelli-Palmarini, Massimo. *Inevitable Illusions: How Mistakes of Reason Rules Our Minds*. New York: Wiley, 1994.

Powell, Esta. "Catharsis in Psychology and Beyond: A Historic Overview." www.primal-page.com/cathar.htm.

Prahalad, C. K., and Gary Hamel. "The Core Competence of the Corporation." *Harvard Business Review*, May–June 1990.

Rad, Gerhard von. *Genesis: A Commentary*. Philadelphia: Westminster, 1972.

Ries, Eric. *The Lean Start-Up: How Today's Entrepreneurs Use Continuous Innovation to Create Radically Successful Businesses*. New York: Crown, 2011.

Rittel, H. W. J., and M. M. Webber. "Dilemmas in a General Theory of Planning." *Policy Sciences*, June 1973.

Rohr, Richard. *Falling Upward: A Spirituality for the Two Halves of Life*. San Francisco: Jossey-Bass, 2011.

Rubenfire, Adam. "CEO's Partly Sunny Economic Outlook." *Wall Street Journal*, July 23, 2014.

Scharmer, C. Otto. *Theory U: Leading from the Future as It Emerges*. San Francisco: Berrett-Koehler, 2009.

Schumpeter, Joseph. *Capitalism, Socialism and Democracy*. New York: Harper, 1942.

Scheff, Thomas J. *Catharsis in Healing, Ritual, and Drama*. Berkeley: University of California Press, 1979.

Schein, Edgar H. "Anxiety of Learning: An Interview with Edgar H. Schein." *Harvard Business Review*, March 2, 2002.

Schon, Donald A. *The Reflective Practitioner: How Professionals Think in Action*. New York: Basic, 1983.

Schwartz, Peter. *The Art of the Long View: Paths to Strategic Insight for Yourself and Your Company*. New York: Doubleday, 1991.

Selman, M. J. "The Kingdom of God in the Old Testament." *Tyndale Bulletin* 40 (1989) 161–83.

Senge, Peter, et al. *Presence: Exploring Profound Change in People, Organizations, and Society*. New York: Random House, 2004.

Skidelsky, Robert, and Edward Skidelsky. *How Much Is Enough: Money and the Good Life*. New York: Other, 2012.

Smith, Adam. *The Glasgow Edition of the Works and Correspondence of Adam Smith*. Edited by R. H. Cambell and A. S. Skinner. Oxford: Clarendon, 1976.

———. *The Theory of Moral Sentiments*. New York: Penguin, 2009. First published 1759.

———. *The Wealth of Nations*. New York: Modern Library, 2000. First published 1776.

Solomon, Andrew. Interview by Terry Gross. "For Sandy Hook Killer's Father, Tragedy Outweighs Love for His Son." Fresh Air, National Public Radio, March 13, 2014.

———. "The Reckoning: The Father of the Sandy Hook Killer Searches for Answers." *New Yorker*, March 17, 2014.

Suzuki, Shunryu. *Zen Mind, Beginner's Mind*. Boston: Shambhala, 2006.

Taleb, Nassim. *The Black Swan: The Impact of the Highly Improbable*. New York: Random House, 2007.

Tanfani, Joseph, and Richard A. Serrano. "Families of Charleston 9 Forgive Shooting Suspect in Court." *Los Angeles Times*, June 19, 2015.

Taylor, Jill Bolte. *My Stroke of Insight: A Brain Scientist's Personal Journey*. New York: Viking, 2008. Material used as basis for TED Talk, February 2008.

Teece, David. "Explicating Dynamic Capabilities: The Nature and Microfoundations of (Sustainable) Enterprise Performance." *Strategic Management Journal* 28 (2007) 1319–50.

Teece, David J., et al. "Dynamic Capabilities and Strategic Management." *Strategic Management Journal* 18 (1997) 509–33.

Kittel, Gerhard, and Gerhard Friedrich, eds. *Theological Dictionary of the New Testament.* Edited and translated by Geoffrey W. Bromiley. 10 vols. Grand Rapids: Eerdmans, 1964.

Tillich, Paul. *Systematic Theology.* Vol. 1. Chicago: University of Chicago Press, 1971.

Turkle, Sherry. *Alone Together: Why We Expect More from Technology and Less from Each Other.* New York: Basic, 2011.

———. *Reclaiming Conversations: The Power of Talk in a Digital Age.* New York: Penguin, 2015.

Utterback, James M. *Mastering the Dynamics of Innovation: How Companies Can Seize Opportunities in the Face of Technological Change.* Boston: Harvard Business School Press, 1994.

Vincent, Lanny. "Innovation Midwives: Sustaining Innovation Streams in Established Companies." *Research-Technology Management*, January–February 2005.

———. *Prisoners of Hope: How Engineers and Others Get Lift for Innovating.* Indianapolis: Westbow, 2011.

Warren, Rick. *The Purpose Driven Life: What on Earth Am I Here For?* Grand Rapids: Zondervan, 2002.

Weick, Karl E. *Sensemaking in Organizations.* Thousand Oaks, CA: SAGE, 1995.

Wilson, Frank R. *The Hand: How Its Use Shapes the Brain, Language and Human Culture.* New York: Vintage, 1999.

Wink, Walter. *The Human Being: Jesus and the Enigma of the Son of the Man.* Minneapolis: Fortress, 2002.

Wladawsky-Berger, Irving. "Some Advice on How to Jump Start Entrepreneurship and Job Creation." *CIO Journal / Wall Street Journal*, November 7, 2014.

World Council of Churches. "The Nature and Mission of the Church: A Stage on the Way to a Common Statement" (2005). Faith and Order Paper 198.

Yeats, W. B. "The Second Coming." In *The Norton Anthology of Modern Poetry*, edited by Richard Ellmann and Robert O'Clair. New York: Norton, 1973.

Zeleny, M. "Management Support Systems: Towards Integrated Knowledge Management." *Human Systems Management* 7 (1987) 59–70.

Made in the USA
San Bernardino, CA
04 December 2017